12-14-72

CHRISTIANS AND
MENTAL HEALTH

CHRISTIANS
AND
MENTAL HEALTH
SAMUEL SOUTHARD

BROADMAN PRESS
NASHVILLE, TENNESSEE

DEDICATION

To the memory of my father,

Samuel Southard

who stored up treasures of
acceptance and adequacy
for children and
children's children

PREFACE

From the mental health perspective, it is quite obvious that a clergyman concerned with mental health is a man involved with basic human values and the broader range of social problems.

The list of such concerns is long, for it includes an abysmal family of interrelated problems: <u>alcoholism</u> and <u>alcohol abuse</u>, <u>crime</u> and <u>delinquency</u>, <u>drug</u> and <u>narcotic abuse</u>, minorities problems, racism, individual and mass violence, sexuality problems, suicide and depression, and youth problems.

These modern issues of mental health/mental illness range from problems capable of solutions from science to those which lie at the heart of man's value system, where religion dwells.

Mental health matters to clergymen because mental health depends upon the values which the individual establishes for himself—and religion is inextricably engaged in this struggle, consciously or unconsciously.

Religion is based on respect for the dignity of the individual, on self-determination, and on adequate opportunities for all individuals. The clergyman has as his domain both illness and health, both the individual and life—the quality of life. Clergymen can offer a dynamism—a commitment to the eradication of misery—to the improving of lives.

A good psychiatrist, particularly one concerned with community psychiatry, is and should be something of a preacher and a politician. And, preachers, of course, can never be above being involved in a little politics, now and then, for the right causes, and thus, also involved even more intimately in the whole business of mental health and mental illness.

BERTRAM S. BROWN, M.D.
Director
National Institute of Mental Health

CONTENTS

CHRISTIANS AND MENTAL HEALTH

CHAPTER I
THE CHALLENGE OF
A MORAL MOVEMENT

Christianity and mental health are personal reactions to life-changing events. One begins with the cross and the resurrection. The other starts with any crucial venture in life.

All these events are grounded in human experience. Feelings and attitudes, behavior and thought are the subject matter of both religion and health. But what are we thinking or feeling about? The answer to that question separates the two movements. Christianity is thought about God. It is the interpretation of events that were crowned with a cross. Mental health is a systematic understanding of man. There is no one saving event, no commanding attitude. Each person writes his story from the common experiences of mankind.

Christianity and mental health are moral movements because they call for personal response to a system of values. People are challenged to accept an interpretation of life that is consistent with principles or goals. All people are asked to live by these principles. Society is shaped by them.

The moral nature of both movements can be seen in the questions they ask.

(1) What does a person live for?

(2) How am I to know myself?

(3) What are my obligations to others?

(4) How can I achieve personal satisfaction and still make a contribution to society?

(5) How can I find acceptance and still be an individual?

(6) What am I to do with guilt and shame?

These and other questions are common to American religion and mental health. If the answers are as similar as the questions, we could start from either movement and obtain the same results.

Such a synthesis seems easy today. On the one hand, many clergymen are uncomfortable with any supernatural emphasis. They are glad to ally themselves with the power of science. Humanism makes sense to them as it does to millions of Americans. They ask why not encourage a person toward mental health without the confusion of vague theological ideas?

On the other hand, mental health workers welcome the meeting of the two movements. They desire the support of churches in the development of mental health clinics. Clergymen are considered valuable allies. Church groups are natural forums for discussions of healthy family life and other preventive programs.

But there are some problems in this alliance. First, the historic purposes of religion are lost. Man and his needs occupy the center stage. God becomes an inconvenience unless he can be explained as the product of a lively imagination.

Mental health workers raise this question more frequently than the clergymen who work with them. A clinical psychologist asked me: "Why don't the chaplains in our hospitals become counselors and have a clear identity? As it is, they explain away so many traditional beliefs that their God is no more than my idea of man. I may be wrong, but at least I am honest with the patients about what I believe. Couldn't we find a minister somewhere who would stand up for the patients' religion?"

The Clinic Next Door

What is to happen when the supernatural element in religion has been eclipsed by the natural power of a scientific movement? Ecclesiastical leaders have often solved this problem by rejecting "modernistic" clergymen. This negative solution is not enough. Many laymen, in and out of the church, are also thinking that mental health comes first. A positive set of ideas about Christianity and mental health is needed. We need to ask, How are human needs related to divine commands?

Another reason for positive church action is the growth of community mental health centers. These centers offer trained personnel for counseling and guidance. They relate scientific finds on health to everyday problems of living through lectures, films, seminars, and personal conversations with people in all walks of life. The question arises, Can the local church match this effort?

Mental health is now becoming as organized as Christianity. This is inevitable. The successful presentation of a moral system leads to power in society. Health is now a major force by virtue of concerned, trained personnel, buildings and budgets that are second only to national defense. When state, Federal, and local funds pour millions of dollars into health facilities for one community, that's power. In a ten-year period, the Federal Government will offer more than one billion dollars of support for community clinics in rural and urban America. State governments spend up to a third of their mental health budgets on such centers.

The Federal Government budgets more for health services than any other domestic program. Mental health is becoming a large part of that budget, and community mental health centers are visible extensions of that concern in many communities.

The days are passing when a poorly paid social worker or a footsore public health nurse carried the professional health needs of fifty thousand people. In the next decade a community of that size might have fifty workers in a well-organized and funded comprehensive health care center. These are the people who will call upon pastors and church leaders for support of health programs and service to people in need. The professionals will be eager to train volunteers from churches and consult with pastors. The question is, Will clergy and churches have the philosophy and dedication to work with this new resource for healing?

Mental Health Comes Home

We will see these professionals in our hometowns because spending for mental health is being reversed. Until 1963, most Federal and state budgets concentrated upon hospitals. Many of these were custodial in nature and removed from population centers. Beginning in 1963, Congress appropriated funds to encourage the study of neighborhood centers in each state. The secretary of Health, Education and Welfare told a House committee: "The National program for mental health is centered on a wholly new emphasis and approach-care and treatment of most mentally ill persons in their own home community." [1]

The new programs will not only be next door, they will also provide education for every home. The first goal of comprehensive community mental health centers is education to teach people the principles of mental hygiene and growth. Prevention is primary. A second goal is education for community leaders. Ministers, doctors, school counselors, public health nurses, policemen, and other public servants are to be trained as a first line of defense against mental illness.

The staff of a community center serve as consultants to the professionals who are already known in the community. The consultation goes beyond help with individual cases to include planning for broad and efficient treatment programs through every agency.

The center staff does some specific evaluations and counseling. A smaller center of two or three professionals could offer little more than evaluation and occasional conversations with people who came in for help. Larger centers may have fifty staff members. Some of these are in the psychiatric service of a general hospital. Others man a day-care center for persons who need guided activities and group discussion but who can go home in the evenings.

The staff is also interested in the rehabilitation of persons who have been hospitalized. They would hope to establish foster home placements, half-way houses, and programs for home visits.

A comprehensive center is interested in a wide range of treatment facilities. Some may be for the chronically mentally crippled, some for alcohol and drug abuse, some for the mentally retarded.

Finally, the Federal regulations for these centers include a requirement for training and research. The staff is to prepare people in the community for service to others and aid the community in understanding why there are barriers to mental health. How can the structure of the community be changed to produce more abundant life and better care?

The mental health center is not only in the community, it is an agent for community change. It is responsible for identifying the needs of an area, the planning of strategy, the development and coordination of resources for mental health.

These are complex programs, which will multiply in town and city throughout the nation. They will offer a vigorous challenge to the church as a healing organization and to the claims of Christian love.

How can the theory and practice of religion make a contribution to community health and maintain a God-consciousness? To find answers, we will first examine the relation of Christian theory to personal practice. What does faith really mean in modern life?

NOTES

1. Raymond Glasscote, et. al., *The Community Mental Health Center* (Washington, D.C., American Psychiatric Association, 1969).

CHAPTER II
WHAT IS MENTAL HEALTH?

Health is a by-product of godly living. It is not an end in itself. The Sermon on the Mount contains this conclusion: "But seek first his kingdom and his righteousness, and all these things shall be yours as well" (Matt. 6:33). Food, health, clothing, and length of life are important, but they are not our ultimate concern. Obedience to God orders everything else in life.

Once the focus of life is established, health and happiness are in place. "All these things" are significant in Christianity. The Model Prayer of Jesus contains a request for daily bread and the ability to forgive those who have wronged us. Neither physical nor social needs are denied. But they come after the request that the kingdom of God becomes a reality on earth.

Mental health is a by-product of surrender to values higher than ourselves. This is the opinion of psychiatrists as well as theologians. A New York psychoanalyst, Gotthard Booth, has said that people stay healthy as long as they are productive. A person must feel that he is pursuing purposes that are vital to him. These purposes must be socially acceptable. He can keep going with a purpose in life even though his problems might handicap a different personality.

By contrast, says Dr. Booth, illness is a state in which a man cannot live up to the demands of living. One sign of illness is a shift of interest from the world to the self. The ill person is preoccupied with how he feels, what he does. "I" is everything.

Victor Frankl has added to this definition of health. From his experience in a Nazi concentration camp, he found that men died without a purpose in life. When he returned to psychiatric practice in Vienna, he began to ask one great question of his patients, "What can you contribute to life?" That is the question of illness. Self-seeking is a sign of sickness.

These psychiatrists are not saying that *concern* for the self is sin. They spend long hours with patients who need to understand themselves better. They find many persons who have disregarded their personal needs of a human being.

The psychiatrists are saying that a person cannot make himself the *center* of life. He is a social being, created to live with and help others. Unless he can think of something beyond himself, he has failed as a human being. The goal of therapy is self-understanding for service.

What is mental health? It is an interpretation of life. The great question is, what can I offer to others? When a person knows that he can make a contribution and begins to make it, he is healthy.

Problems People Face

Mental health is an interpretation of *events* in life. There are crucial experiences that change us. Early home training, the first days in school, the making of friendships, courtship, marriage, children, sickness, and death are building stones or stumbling blocks to each individual. Mental health is strengthened or diminished by the significant events of life. They have a permanent and a temporary effect upon our ability to cope with life.

The permanent effect is called character. We see the results in many ways. A person who was surrounded by love during every experience of life will probably trust people. He will be open and friendly to others. Conversely, persons who have been exploited by associates and misused by parents since childhood will be closed and suspicious. The lack of affection has left permanent damage.

The temporary effect of an event may not be so damaging. The event may be betrayal in adulthood by a close friend or business associate. For a period of days or weeks the person who is hurt may withdraw from others and suspect the motives of those who talk with him. But if his basic health is good, the wound will heal and he will distinguish between betrayal by one person and distrust of the entire world. There are occasions when events beyond our control will have a depressing effect upon us. Just as employment in a sought after job will bring us a sense of elation, so the loss of a job will bring the anxiety of financial insecurity and perhaps a sense of failure. These may be short-term problems. The longer term of despair may come through war experience. Combat veterans may need months to regain the sense of joy and freedom with others that characterized their life before combat.

Mental health is really a balance of events and their interpretations by individuals. Because there are so many changes in events and attitudes, we cannot measure health at one time alone. Health is a state of being. When we say that a person is healthy, we mean that on most occasions he handles the relationships of life with maturity. We do not mean that he is always healthy, anymore than we would speak of another person as always ill.

The ups and downs of illness and health are often pointed out to visitors in psychiatric institutions. One may complain to a staff member, "These patients look and act just as sane as I am." The staff member may say: "They certainly are when you see them, and we hope they will be that way for longer periods of time. But, some of them lose control of their emotions whenever they go back home or try to get a job. So long as they remain in this sheltered environment, they make a good adjustment. Our problem is to strengthen them for adjustment in the outside world."

The goal of psychotherapy is to strengthen resources for health over the damaging effects of illness. There will be times when a person sinks down into depression or erupts in a rage. If these are infrequent and do not lead to the loss of a job or family, we would call the person healthy. Generally he has control of his feelings.

The Meaning of Healthy Adjustment

One test of mental health is the ability of an individual to weather a storm of life. If he cannot cope with a crisis, he may become ill. Illness and health may then be described as reactions to stress. One person makes a satisfactory adjustment, another fails.

How do people adjust to life? When more than two thousand Americans were asked that question in 1960, they gave two kinds of answers.

The first answer to adjustment is happiness. Most Americans think they are well adjusted when they feel happy. The source of happiness is very important. Happy marriages, for example, concentrate on relationships. People describe the joy of being with each other. The less happy marriages concentrate on an active social life, a well-equipped house or well-behaved children.

Men are happy when their job means something. A significant place in the organization is more important than the amount of money they receive. Sometimes a man expresses more satisfaction with his job than with his marriage. He can *do* something at work which people can see and approve. He may not *be* the kind of person that a wife or children would enjoy.

Happy persons have worries but they are temporary. There will be a time when money is short, husband or wife is ill, or children misbehave. The happy persons have hope that these problems can be solved. Usually they have emotional or financial resources to fight for health.

When a person is consumed by worry we see a different picture. This is the second general word for adjustment, "worry." It is a chronic way of life for people who have little hope. The people who were in most despair during the survey were the wives of unemployed day laborers. Neither husband nor wife had any investment to make in life. Their energies were consumed in a daily struggle for existence.

A better job or education would give hope to some of these chronic worriers. But others are caught in a vicious way of thinking. They plan so poorly that life is one crisis after another. They make such impulsive decisions that money is spent on unessentials and the loan sharks move in. Husbands and wives take out their frustrations on each other rather than leaning on each other for support. These persons are in desperate need of some third party who can teach them a better way of life adjustment.

Adjustment to life is explained in terms of (1) happiness or gratification and (2) investment in life. Both of these are essential for mental health. A person must believe that he is making a contribution to the world, and he must gain personal satisfaction from the contribution that he makes.

A New Emphasis in Treatment

Professional and financial resources are now available to practice these definitions of mental health. Community centers can provide education and support for better adjustments to life. People can get help during a crisis and recover their psychic equilibrium before permanent damage is done.

The purpose of mental health clinics is to tip the balance toward health. When more professional help is available, people take hope. Something can be done about problems before they reach crisis proportions. The presence of these experts in a community will help us see the sources of happiness and unhappiness. For many people, the "problem" is in people rather than in things. The solution involves attitudes, habits, behavior, and character.

As we meet more and more workers in the field of health, we will develop a new sensitivity to everyday problems. These problems are expressed as worry about children, lack of affection from husband, status seeking by wife, insensitivity of employer, lack of understanding from parents. These are the issues of life that can be handled hopefully and creatively before a person is beaten down into despair or illness. The emphasis can be upon prevention more than upon cure.

When cure is necessary because of illness, it can be different from the former days of custodial treatment in a faraway hospital. Help can be found near home in outpatient services, hospitalization during the day, and clinics for care after treatment. There are enough professional workers in clinics to talk with all members of a family, so there can be some emphasis upon the way people relate to each other. In former days, the patient might be counseled to act in a different way with another member of the family, but nothing was done with the other family members. Now there is the possibility of talking with all the adults and with older children as well.

The results of this shift in emphasis can be dramatic. Some state mental hospitals have less than a third of the patients they housed ten years ago. The development of mental health clinics in one city may cut the flow of patients to hospitals in half. In addition, the instruction that is offered to school teachers with behavior problems, to ministers with problem parishioners, to policemen with delinquents will extend the strength of helping persons far beyond the range of a clinic or hospital. The goal is to prevent people from coming either to clinic or to hospital.

Of course, the goal will not be reached. The mental health movement will not solve all the problems of society. Families may decide they are not going to accept some of these new ideas about living. Individuals will still suffer stress that leads to illness or endure chronic unhappiness and worry.

What we can say is that more trained people are available to help those who will listen and support those who take action toward a better way of life.

Some clinics have been so successful in reducing the flow of patients to mental hospitals that anything seems possible with enough money and personnel. There is great danger in this grand hope. A community clinic should lay more emphasis upon community than clinic. The secret of survival is in work through well-established leaders rather than imported talent. There will be no long-range benefits from a clinic unless there is support from teachers, ministers, doctors, policemen, judges, and politicians.

Do Churches Support Mental Health?

Health workers have been anxious to get church support. They seek ministers to serve on advisory committees. They speak in churches and look to religion as an ally.

What can Christianity say to these new emphases in mental health? Theoretically, we can say a great deal. But it will have to be realistic. First, we must admit the difference between "religion that is pure and undefiled" and the prideful attitudes which often masquerade as religion. There is no help in the hypocrisy, literalism, and slavish conformity to community standards that was denounced by Jesus. No one is helped by a pious concern for form without a love for people. The apostle John bluntly stated: "If anyone says, 'I love God,' and hates his brother, he is a liar" (1 John 4:20).

Christian theology and mental health are one in opposing the pride of traditional morality and conformity to outward standards. These attitudes often hide our contempt for other human beings, including ourselves. Both disciplines, Christian theology and mental health, emphasize humble attitudes more than correct actions. The Hebrew prophets cried, "Rend your hearts and not your garments." When actions do speak louder than words, it is through selfless service that no one may observe.

What does pure and undefiled religion have to offer in the field of mental health?

Christianity has a place for the best and the worst in human experience. We are commanded to weep with those who weep and rejoice with those who rejoice.

Christianity is a religion of deliverance. It allows men to fail in various parts of their lives without feeling that they have failed all over. Sorrow, pain, and personal failure are included in religious experience. Suffering is not explained, but it is transcended through the example of Jesus, who suffered in every way as those who were to follow him.

At the same time, religion can be joyous. Jesus seemed to have such a good time that some religious leaders of his day were scandalized. The reply of the master was that disciples should rejoice while the bridegroom was with them.

The source of happiness is interpersonal. The "blessed" or happy person is one who practices forgiveness, love, and longsuffering. Faith and hope give him power.

The wide range of Christian experience is consistent with the modern emphasis of mental health. Here is a philosophy of life that understands the ups and downs of events and emotions. It is an emphasis upon balance.

Another emphasis of Christianity is upon *being* as well as *doing*. Attitudes are as important as actions. This dual emphasis should be a wholesome corrective to some extremes in psychological theories. Some psychiatrists have overemphasized the Freudian methods of psychoanalysis. There has been such heavy concentration upon work with one patient over a period of months or years that the great majority of people in need were ignored. On the other side, some psychologists ignored individual attitudes and stressed behavior. So long as actions could be shaped in desirable directions they were content.

The classic Christian emphasis has been upon the shaping of behavior and the transformation of attitudes. The book of James proclaims that faith without works is dead. The apostle Paul asked if a man can be saved by righteous actions. Must there not be inner transformation as well? Jesus warned the multitudes that ritual cleansing of utensils was not enough; the "inside of the cup" must also be clean. The goal is a regenerate man in a reformed society.

Social relations are another emphasis of Christian faith. Fellowship is essential. Those who bear one another's burden fulfil the law of Christ. The church is to be a community that cares.

Is this really true? In the next chapters we will look at the evidence for the church as a fellowship of concern and for Christian faith to produce character.

CHAPTER III
DO CHRISTIANS REALLY CARE?

Those who care the most go to church the least. This is the conclusion of a survey of a national sample of about fourteen hundred adult Americans by Milton Rokeach, department of psychology, Michigan State University.

In this survey, thirty-two issues were used to rate compassion. Some of these measured attitudes toward the poor. Should there be free college education for the poor, better housing, guaranteed minimum income, free dental and medical care, increased taxes, additional welfare legislation? Other attitudes were on civil rights. Did Martin Luther King bring on his own death? Should every person have a right to adequate housing? What about interracial marriage? There were questions about student protest and the involvement of the church in contemporary affairs, such as the urban crisis, the war in Vietnam, and civil rights.

According to this survey, the values of churchgoers are different from nonattenders. Religion is considered to be very important in the life of the churchgoers. By religion is meant salvation. This was the value checked first on a list of eighteen "terminal values." Religious people also place a high value on forgiveness and obedience. These were first in a list of "instrumental values."

The nonchurchgoer is more interested in such values as "independent," "intellectual," "logical."

Since those who profess religion give the highest value to salvation and forgiveness, one would think that they would demonstrate the greatest concern for fellowmen. The social and psychological studies of Rokeach and others do not support that assumption. A variety of studies in the last ten years show that Christian values apparently guide man's conduct away from his fellowman. Questionnaires present the religious-minded person as indiffernt to a social system that perpetuates injustice. His only concern seems to be the saving of his soul.[1]

These are harsh judgments. But they should be viewed with caution since the conclusions are drawn from questionnaires. The language of a question may be imperfectly understood, and the range of questions may be inadequate.

But with many studies that reach similar conclusions, what are we to say? Many of us know persons who do fit the conclusions of Rokeach and others. Many churchgoers reacted in a fearful and calloused way to the assassination of Martin Luther King. Many are unsympathetic with the student protest movement and are opposed to the church's involvement in everyday affairs. By some churchgoers, the poor are considered people who have brought misfortune upon themselves.

These conclusions are questionnaire conclusions, but I can sometimes see the same thing in a Sunday School class or in a daily newspaper. In 1970 a Presbyterian pastor in North Georgia admitted that a Head Start program for underpriviledged children was abandoned because the program was refused the use of the church basement during the week. Other facilities in the town had already been refused.

I could hear similar views in the Sunday School classes of wealthy congregations in large cities. In a lesson on the church and poverty, several laymen complained bitterly that able bodied men were sitting idle while they had to work seventy hours a week and pay heavy taxes. When women in the class replied that 90 percent of welfare payments went to the disabled, the widowed, and mothers with small children, the "successful" businessmen would not listen.

Another church sponsored a seminar on youth and drugs. One woman said: "Young people need some time to think out their reason for living in this bewildering world. Some of them experiment with drugs while they are trying to figure out their place in life. I don't like the drugs, but I am sympathetic with their drop out from society for a while."

Two men bitterly rejected this statement. "I can't stand to see those freaks sitting on the sidewalk, doing nothing. They should be made to work." The lady replied: "Isn't thinking hard work?" "Not their way of thinking!" replied one man. The other man took up the argument: "What we are saying is that people who won't work aren't worth our money. Why should I pay taxes for an expensive welfare program that supports all those hippies?" Another woman replied: "But those young people are not on welfare, they're living off their fathers bankbook, their own money, or each other." "That's just the point," shouted one man, "A man's not worth anything if he doesn't pay taxes."

Are these views prevalent in your church? They were typical enough in this church for some men of compassion to drop out. A doctor who was concerned about young people on drugs had been teaching a Sunday School class. He tried to enlist the help of adult sponsors for various projects with runaways, dropouts, and drug users. He met as much hostility in the church as he did in the medical community. Without support from either of those sources, he established a clinic and was soon overwhelmed by young people in need. He reduced his lucrative medical practice and gave up his Sunday School class to help those who needed him the most.

Certainly there are exceptions to this gloomy picture. A businessman in one community bought a house to be used as a haven for runaways and drug users. There have been many women who took the lead in welfare and civil rights programs in town and city.

But the caring minority is often submerged under the calloused majority of churchgoers. Are the questionnaires correct? Are churchgoers compassionate?

How Christian Are Churchgoers?

Is church attendance a reliable measure of Christian faith? The answer depends on what we mean by faith.

On the one hand, Rokeach and others show that a belief in salvation and the importance of religion is closely related to frequent church attendance. Persons who *profess* faith are in church. Furthermore, the frequent church attender will often say that personal salvation is his first concern. He goes to church to worship God. This is his primary objective.

Those who are absorbed in personal salvation may not think of Christian charity in terms of government welfare programs or political movements. Their emphasis upon compassion is individual. Like John Wesley, they would preach repentance to children in the death rows of stinking prisons without involving the church in the political issue of prison reform.

But once a person becomes involved with prisoners or others in need, another definition of Christianity presses upon him. This is the requirement to love his neighbor as himself. Compassion for others is an essential sign of true religion.

For him, the New Testament's definition of faith is love for God *and* man. Concern for neighbor is defined by

Jesus as visitation of the sick and prisoners, clothing and feeding of the poor, hospitality to strangers. To minister to one of the least of these is to minister to Christ himself (Matt. 25:31–46). Christian faith is an open heart toward those who are brokenhearted.

This definition of Christian faith will clash with those churchgoers who want salvation without sacrifice. A concern for the poor and needy might lead to a loss of status. Who wants to be identified with the outcast of society? Psychological studies have recently demonstrated what perceptive Christians have known for a long time—many who say "Lord, Lord" are not in the kingdom. Gordon Allport of Harvard University found that a majority of churchgoers were "yes sayers." They agreed with everything good about religion and everything that seemed good for them in society. Since good in society meant middle-class white status they rejected minority groups. They were for everything that looked popular.

If a church took a stand against culture, the "yes sayers" would drop away. There is no place in their philosophy of life for risks, unpopularity, courage. Their cry to the church is "don't rock the boat." To them, Christianity is like an ark in which they are secure from the threats of life. They have no idea of Christian faith as a pilgrimage through a hostile land.

Allport found a minority of churchgoers who thought of faith in terms of courage and sacrifice. These persons believed that the worship of God required something of them. They were not satisfied with social and material security. These were secondary to their spiritual loyalties.

The Churches' Barrier to the Brokenhearted

Care for the fatherless and widows is a New Testament criteria of true religion. Could a person show this concern toward individuals without supporting social programs for the welfare of needy persons? The answer is a qualified yes. The religion and the culture of a region may condition a person to react against organized programs for social service. The American tradition of self-reliance is still strong in some places.

But personal contact with those in need has usually changed this emphasis. Those who believed in rugged individualism have been so stirred by the plight of underpriviledged people that political and government action seemed mandatory. In modern times, it is not enough to pass a cup of cold water to an individual. If the water is polluted, a Christian must be involved in political and economic movements.

An exclusive emphasis upon salvation is only a temporary barrier to care for those in need. As soon as the saved person becomes involved in the problems of his community, he is caught up in the full dimension of salvation. Individual and social action are a part of his new commitment.

The permanent barrier to compassion is hardness of heart. Those who cannot forgive, cannot love. This is so essential that Jesus made it a part of his Model Prayer for his diciples. God's forgiveness of us and our forgiveness of one another are a part of the same sentence in that prayer.

Jesus taught the relationship of forgiveness and compassion in many ways. For example, when he was in the home of Simon the Pharisee, a woman of the city, who was a sinner, began to wet his feet with her tears and wipe them with the hair of her head and annointed his feet with ointment.

Turning to his host, Jesus told the story of a creditor who forgave two men. One had a large debt, the other a small one. Who loved the creditor more?

"The one, I suppose, to whom he forgave more," said Simon.

Jesus then contrasted the attentive treatment he had received from the woman with the lack of courtesy from Simon. He provided no water for bathing nor a towel. These were the common courtesies of the day. The woman who was a sinner did far more than this. Why? Because her sins were forgiven.

Two lessons come from this story. First, those who care the most have been forgiven the most. They know the meaning of the saying, "We love because he first loved us." Their hearts are open to the suffering of others because they have known remorse, guilt, and failure. Now their burdens have been lifted, and they can share freely with others the joy of their deliverance.

The second lesson is that values are revealed by that to which we give devotion and allegiance. Simon showed by his actions that Jesus was unimportant. The woman who was a sinner made him the very center of her life.

That which claims our time and attention is what we live by. The person who has time for the poor, the sick, the prisoners has shown that Christ is at the center of his devotion. The person who pays no attention to the outcast is greatly surprised to find that they should be the center of his religious life. He thought that it was enough to look toward God in church.

Some Contemporary Surprises

Jesus surprised the religious people of his day by linking true religion to the plight of helpless and hurt people. Similar shocks are in store for many churchmen today.

The greatest eye-opener is that people still look to churches for help with the failures of life. A national survey has shown that when people are in emotional distress, they turn to a minister more than to any other professional person in the community. One reason for this may be his availability. There are more ministers than doctors, psychologists, or psychiatrists, and they are more widely distributed throughout the United States.

But that is only part of the answer. People turn to ministers because religion is still believed to be a refuge for the troubled in spirit, the confused, and the depressed. The public believes that Christians *should* care. They have heard that Christ came to preach deliverance to the captive, to bind up the wounds of the brokenhearted. They expect the disciples of the master to live as he did.

The surprises to churchgoers will increase with each

new government aid program. These have steadily increased since World War II. First there was the government campaign to reduce political oppression of minority groups. This culminated in a public call from President Johnson upon churches to lead the way toward desegregation and civil rights. Most local congregations were unprepared for any action on racial injustice. Most were silent. A few made headlines when they turned black visitors away from worship services. There was accuracy in the complaint of many churchmen: "We were getting along just fine before the government interfered." That is, the indifference of the church was not challenged in the past. Now a powerful agent in society was saying: "You do something with us about this moral problem."

Then came the war on poverty. Again, many churches were surprised to find that the poor and the underprivileged wanted to use the empty classrooms of downtown churches. In some instances there was cooperation between the people who lived near the church and the members who had fled to the suburbs. The churches were opened for weekday activities. But in other instances, the churches avoided the opportunity or rejected the request that came.

The barriers in many churches are both physical and spiritual. The members will open neither their church doors nor their hearts to those who are in need.

Now there is a new challenge in mental health and mental retardation. Added to this are new programs in alcohol and drug addiction treatment. Some church leaders have responded by inviting speakers from these programs to meet with their people. Ministers have accepted invitations to serve on the local boards of control. Some members have spoken in city councils for funds to support these clinics and others have raised private resources.

What will happen when the mental health clinics create more specific demands for concern from the churches? Will congregations provide volunteers for the care and reeducation of mentally retarded children? Will there be a place in Sunday School for those who have been chronically mentally ill and now can come home? How about the use of religious education facilities during the week for seminars with working mothers or group meetings of Alcoholics Anonymous?

When we get specific, the churches often fail. The contrast between the teachings of Christ and the requirement of discipleship are too great for many to bear. For example, one congregation was moved by eloquent pleas of the pastor to accept denominational funds for a retarded children's kindergarten. A part of the program was a monthly meeting of parents with the Christian education staff of the church. Out of these meetings came an interest on the part of some parents in church attendance. There was also some movement for a special Sunday School class for retarded children.

As the socially outcast and their parents came into closer contact with the church and its program, opposition grew among church leaders. Several complained that church property would be damaged. Others said that too much money was being spent on a social problem. The most telling argument was: "These are just not our kind of people." The social class was not a barrier. The barrier was failure. In the eyes of church leaders, these parents were not successful. They had a retarded child.

After a year, the congregation refused to accept any more funds from the denomination for a continuation of the program. At the same time, the church refused to lease some educational space for a government-sponsored program for retarded children. The government officials were bewildered. The kindergarten run by the church had attracted such favorable attention in the community that the community now wanted to offer larger support. Church leaders were alarmed by the community interest. The emphasis of their congregation must *not* be upon the "little ones" of the world.

Within two years, the discouraged pastor had accepted a state government position that gave him power and resources to aid handicapped people throughout the state. He is respected in the secular world for a work that was rejected in the church.

The leadership of such congregations will steadfastly say: "The business of the church is to save souls and develop individual character." Some of them will be greatly surprised to find that God is interested in more than their narrow definition of religion.

NOTES
1. Rodney Stark, "Rokeach Religion and Reviewers, Keeping an Open Mind," *Review of Religious Research,* Vol. II, No. 2, p. 152.

CHAPTER IV
CHARACTER OR PERSONALITY?

Caring for others is a sign of mature character. It is a central virtue of adulthood. Church and clinic have had different views of character. One starts with moral expectations. The other begins with scientific explanations. Moral theologians talk about virtues. Psychologists speak of personal characteristics. "Characteristics" are morally neutral. They are only descriptions. But "character" implies standards of ethics. It sounds judgmental.

Most mental health workers have been trained to avoid "value judgments." They do not believe that their standards of conduct should be imposed upon clients. The traditional psychiatric question has been: "What do *you* want to do?"

This emphasis has been valuable to people in conflict

with their own standards. Clients have been helped to see what is required of them by society, what they have been taught by parents, what their own desires may be. When these three elements of decision-making are related, the person can exercise better judgment. The final decision is left with him.

To emphasize ethical neutrality, mental health workers have used the term personality rather than character. Personality is a more descriptive phrase. It suggests visible behavior, appearance, measurable traits.

A descriptive emphasis was possible when most counseling took place in a university clinic or hospital. The patient was separated from his natural environment, including his family. He was treated in a scientific atmosphere where his behavior and attitudes could be observed and explained. Any evaluation was made in terms that minimized traditional morality. The scientist wished to be as objective as possible. Neither his culture nor that of the client should distort diagnosis and treatment.

The force of community mental health has broken this scientific isolation. Clients now live at home rather than in a hospital. They bring the culture into the clinic with them. The professional worker may now live in a community which shares the values of his clients. He no longer lives in a separate compound on the hospital grounds or in the university housing of large cities. The worker, his wife, and his family are exposed to the school, the church, the government, the business that radiate the moral expectations of a culture.

Of course, the professional person may live in a different *section* of town from many of his clients. This separation is questioned by some in the field of mental health. They want both the clinic and the staff to be physically in the areas of greatest need. If professional staff members live in a different section, then most of the other workers should be drawn from the neighborhood of a clinic. These are the "indigenous" mental health workers.

In addition to a physical neighborliness, some mental health workers are also insisting upon the control of clinics by neighbors. If services are provided in an Italian ward, then representatives from that ward should be on a local board of control. If a clinic is located in a ghetto, minority spokesmen in that area should be on the committees that say how money will be spent.

How do professional mental health workers respond to these challenges? Many have been prepared in theory for these changes. At scientific meetings they hear demands that policy be based on the community expectations. They also read research on the importance of values in resolving personal and social conflict. Psychologists like Milton Rokeach have shown how long-term goals affect conduct. When he was asked to help unravel the tangled relations of ghetto blacks and white policemen in one city, he soon found a major source of conflict. The two groups fought for different values. The blacks put freedom at the top of their list. Policemen emphasized control and responsibility. How could the groups work together when they had such different commitments?

Values must be explored before social conflicts can be resolved. The same emphasis is being made in individual therapy. Mental health workers are being urged to identify what they stand for. They gain respect from clients when their ideals are clear. Also, they must take actions consistent with the goals they have for themselves and others. William Glasser has demonstrated this in his work with young people in trouble. In "reality therapy" he not only tells a youth what he expects; he backs it up with administrative decision. Privileges are lost for misconduct. Rewards are given for character-building behavior. The young people respond with respect. They have found an adult who cares enough to commit himself.

As a result of new professional teaching and the requirements of community centers, professionals are more willing to state their goals and act on them. Ethical standards are becoming a visible part of therapy. This is true both in conversation about attitudes and in observation of conduct.

The control of conduct is now being systematized through "behavior modification." Mental health workers meet with a group of patients to determine the behavior that would be helpful and harmful to the group. The behavior is specified and a reward or punishment attached to it. A supervisor rates each person in the group on a daily basis and publishes the results for all to see.

For example, young persons who were mentally retarded had been living in a house near an institution where they worked. Their work was supervised in preparation for their move into a job on their own. There were problems for the houseparents, such as noise and lights until early in the morning, poor appearance on the part of some young people, bad language, or careless table manners.

A psychologist sat down with the houseparents and the young people to discuss better ways of living. This was considered valuable both as preparation for permanent employment and for happy relations in the house. A list of acceptable behaviors were printed and each young person was given a score at the end of the day. Those with a high score were given more privileges while those with a low score were restricted. The result was a happier community of people and a more impressive appearance before present and potential employers.

The Psychological Sources of Character

Character is personality evaluated by ethical and cultural standards. These standards are often named virtues. They are qualitative descriptions of an individual. When we link description with quality, we have combined character and personality.

The psychological side of character has been called personality development. It is an emphasis upon the accomplishments of socially acceptable tasks at the time when a person is biologically and emotionally equipped to face that requirement. Honesty, for example, can be taught when a child is old enough to know the difference between fantasy and reality. Toilet training can be rewarding when timed with physical control of the bladder. Obedience to rules and team spirit can be related to a twelve-year-old's ambition to get along with playmates.

When the accomplishment of a task is related to a goal in life, we see a virtue developing. Virtues are visible signs of inherent strength. They identify an active quality of life. They can be identified with stages in life development. The virtues of one stage are stepping stones toward maturity. This is the way they have been described by Erik Erikson in *Insight and Responsibility.*

The virtue of childhood is hope. It is an enduring belief that our most fervent wishes are possible despite the fears and frustrations of early years. Hope is nurtured by trustworthy persons. From parents and others we learn that the world is a friendly place. We can believe in others because they have met our basic needs.

Untrustworthy parents and relatives lead a child to distrust others as he grows older. As an adult, such a damaged person does not believe that the world is friendly. He is continually suspicious and cynical. His character is defective because he lacks a primary virtue.

Willpower, or fortitude, is another fruit of childhood experience. It is the unbroken determination to exercise freedom of choice as well as restraint of the self. Fortitude grows out of acceptance and frustration. A child knows that he is wanted and loved by his parents. He also knows that there are limitations. He must restrain his own urges to gain social approval. He must exchange willfulness for good will.

Later in childhood, competence emerges. In time this

will become pride of workmanship. It is a sense of satisfaction in doing a job well. The virtue of work is built up by the concern and attention of those who are important to us. It may be the time that a parent spends in helping to tie a shoe. Later it may be instruction in games or supervision in tasks in the yard or in the house.

When significant people show us this attention and give of themselves in training, we have motivation for achievement and inner standards of workmanship. Without this time and attention, we defeat ourselves through ignorance and inferiority. We do not believe our work is competent and we are robbed of satisfaction.

The great virtue of adolescence is fidelity. It is a sustained loyalty to purposes beyond ourselves. We express it through identification with a group who shares these values. This is the cornerstone of adult identity. It is set in place by the approval of peers and the support of adults. We pledge our allegiance to that which others accept and we do not fall away when powerful persons contradict what we have accepted.

Without sustained loyalties, a person is split apart. He can make no permanent decisions about marriage, work, or leisuretime activities. He has not found himself because he does not know how to give himself.

When a person has freely given himself to others, he has achieved the highest virtue, love. This is mutual devotion that subdues the antagonisms that separate people. It is the deliberate choice of one person to invest himself forever in another.

The result of love is care for others. This virtue of charity is expressed as a widening concern for the family of man. Those who care are cared for. In adult life they have the satisfaction of knowing that they are significant to other people. Their works and their ideas are important to family, friends, and co-laborers. Without this reinforcement, adults cannot generate concern beyond the narrow circle of family and friends. There must be inner drive and outer challenge to continually produce beyond our basic satisfactions.

But man can only produce so much. He must learn when to simplify, when to place one value above another. This is the virtue of wisdom. It is the choice of what is best in the face of death.

Hypocrisy and Hostility

When goals in life are related to stages of development, we can minimize the dangers of hypocrisy. Hypocrisy assumes a crown without a cross. Men think they can say "Lord, Lord" without the hard work of discipleship.

A person is made righteous, but he earns virtue. Character must be built. Without the labor, there can be no label.

The building must be systematic. Hypocrisy not only separates profession from practice, it isolates one virtue from another. One man magnifies courage and neglects charity. The result is cruelty.

Developmental psychology has helped us to understand this part of hypocrisy. One virtue may have developed because personal resources were adequate at that stage in development. But a person might be deprived of parents, peers, or approving persons at some later stage in life. His character would be unfinished.

Religion has often refused to accept these psychological limitations. Moral theologians have asserted that willpower can overcome any defect. The result is unnatural. Men affirm what they are not because someone else assumes it is instantly possible.

Simon Peter was the first example of this. He assumed a perfect loyalty to Christ. But Jesus warned him that in the threatening days of his trial, Simon would fall away with all the rest. It took personal humiliation, repentance and divine grace for Simon Peter to learn his lesson. A disciple does not become loyal and loving by an instant act of the will.

This assertion will be offensive to self-assured people who live by rigid standards. They assume that conscious intention can produce inner change. They are especially concerned about the control of hostility. Hate must be subdued by relentless willpower, they say.

Hate checked by will is still hyprocrisy. Outer controls may be strong, while inner desires rage. Jesus saw this in some religious people of his day. They despised the sick and the poor, but they did not openly abuse them. Instead, they stood silently around Jesus when he asked them if he should heal the withered hand of a man on the sabbath day. Was it right to do good or evil on the sabbath? The religious people were so frozen in their hate that they could not answer him a word.

Jesus looked at them with anger, grieved at the hardness of their hearts. His love for those in need was frustrated by the malice of those who sought to destroy him.

Love makes the difference between anger and hatred. When our desire to help others is frustrated by evil, we become angry. It is a temporary emotion that is related to a specific event or attitude.

Hostility is a long-term feeling that may become the major characteristic of a personality. It is nurtured by deprivation in the past and triggered by reminders of the past in the present.

The cure for hatred is a love that can reach back into the past and fill up the need for acceptance in the present. The key to the past is forgiveness. A person cannot *will* forgiveness. It is a divine gift. The medicine of grace moves slowly to heal the scar of hostility that has deep roots.

There can be conscious control of anger because it is related to present events. We can speak of willpower as a valuable ally of anger. But hatred, the desire to plot and destroy, is a power beyond immediate control. Surrender to a power beyond ourselves is the remedy.

It is hypocritical to pretend that we can smother hostility. Our motives are detected. We may stand silent while someone helps those whom we hate, but then we will go away and plot the destruction of the healer.

Psychological studies have helped us distinguish between the long-term development of hostility and the healthy surge of anger which can be controlled. With this insight, we can understand the meaning of Paul's admonition to be angry but not sin. The sin is hostility, a chronic condition that yields only to gradual healing of love.

The Religious Ideal

The development of character has been strengthened by the careful studies of psychologists, psychiatrists, sociologists, and educators. These are all experts in the sciences of man. What contribution does the knowledge of God, theology, make to our ethical identity?

The first contribution is an ideal. Moral theology has formulated the best characteristics of a man. These have been based on personal observations, religious teaching, philosophical systems. The result is a series of descriptions that could fit the highest aspirations of western man. Psychiatrists are now asking their patients, what can you give to life? Moral theology has labeled some of these gifts: faith, hope, love, prudence, fortitude, justice.

When the ideal is related to character development, life's tasks and transcendent goals are realistic. Our problem has not been with the classic ideals of moral theology, but with the magical assumption that we could be such persons by an act of the will. But saying the words do not make it so.

Closely related to the formulation of ideals is the idea of the classical. It is a viewpoint that guides our description, selection, and presentation of personal characteristics. The classical description is a golden mean. That is, a seemingly infinite number of observations about personality are reduced to a chosen few. That which is chosen embodies the best of a faith or philosophy. But it is also a "typical" example, it is a life that any person in the culture might develop.

The thought forms and labels of classic virtues are valuable in any age. They become the common designations of characteristics for people of different generations, social classes, and background. When accepted by a culture, they are reliable descriptions of individuals.

The mental health movement needs these classic ideals for community communication. Citizens are usually friendly to new professionals in a town, but there is much speculation: I wonder what they are like? Can these strangers be trusted? These questions are especially important when mental health and illness are an issue. Most people are vaguely anxious about this subject. They know little, and what they do know is not comforting. Will these experts stir up trouble? It doesn't take much for rumors to fly around a disturbing topic. Anxiety is contagious.

The sharing of ideals is a bridge across these troubled waters. Love, truthfulness, honesty, courage, humility, loyalty are words of strength. They are values desired by all people. Discussion and demonstration of these virtues will transcend some of the differences of custom or the anxieties of an unknown subject.

When a community has examined and sanctioned the ethics of a new movement, it can grow. But how are the professionals in that movement to know what the town will accept? How can they present their work so that people will understand?

Pastors and church officers are community gatekeepers who answer these questions. They invite guests to the "welcome table." Here there is some exploration of the motives of newcomers. If these are acceptable, there are questions about the best way to get started. If the professionals ask for guidance, old-timers point out the clues that signal acceptance or rejection by a segment of the population.

A high-school teacher gave some clues to a community worker about hostility "uptown." The worker did not wear a coat and tie when he called on several ministers of uptown churches. The clergyman considered this a sign of disrespect. The worker wore shoes "turned inside out," as one businessman called them, to a mental health board meeting. This made the worker a "hippie" to several members.

"But," protested the worker, "I wear these shoes and a sports shirt to identify with the people who come to our clinic. They have been exploited in the past by ministers and insurance salesmen who came around in coat and tie. They see me as one with them. If I'm going to share their problems, I must know what is offensive in dress. Don't the board members want me to get with it out there?"

"Well, yes," said the teacher, "and I'm glad you know what is needed out there. I wouldn't have thought of that. It's a good point, and probably should be made to the board and some other people. But when you go uptown, remember they read you by dress, too. If you look "straight" to them, you're in. You have a good personality."

There are so many little cues that lead to such big conclusions. It may be dress, manner, or language. The question is: "How can I conform in that which is unessential so that I can get across the message that counts?" To answer that question, a new professional needs to know what counts in this community. If he can relate his values to some that are dominant in his new surroundings, he has begun to tap roots.

What are the positive links of a new movement to old customs? The chain is formed by words as well as by actions. Here, mental health is disadvantaged. Diagnostic categories are negative. They refer to illness. There are few professional words for mental *health*. How are the goals of life to be described? What is sound character?

Religion offers a positive description of goals for life. The names of classic virtues are hopeful terms for strength of personality. They are models for all men because they begin in the common conditions of life and rise to ethical heights. Words like faith, hope, charity can belong to all classes and races.

We are just beginning to see these classic descriptions in the field of mental health, through authors like Erik Erickson. He knows the specialized jargon of a profession, but he does not reduce character to "oral," "anal," and "phallic." Imagine the impact of those terms on an unsophisticated audience!

Theology's third contribution is to relate what *is* to

what *ought* to be. Ethics goes beyond character development. Psychologists and psychiatrists may help a patient ask the question: "What can I offer to life?" Religion sets forth the virtues that have been considered worthy offerings by others. Mental health workers can assist a person to strive for meaning in life. Theology describes the kind of life that has meaning here and hereafter.

In addition to a description of those that are worthy, religion also provides motivation toward those goals. Christian faith has promised forgiveness for those who are guilty, so that they may rise up and make a direct contribution to life. Divine love is promised to those who surrender to a higher power. This is the force that breaks through hate. Eternal hope is offered to people who despair in this life. They are sustained and comforted.

Religion is the force that faces death. It deals with the questions that go beyond health and happiness in this world. It offers courage and guidance for the best kind of living in the face of dying.

These are the claims of Christianity. Is too much promised? In the next chapter we will examine the evidence for what God can do.

CHAPTER V
DOES GOD MAKE A DIFFERENCE?

"I am not come to call the righteous, but sinners to repentance." With these words Jesus answered the question: "What difference does God make?" He makes a difference to those who are known in their own eyes as sinners. These are the persons who ask for mercy, forgiveness, newness of life. They must have a power beyond themselves to heal broken lives. Human strength is not sufficient.

In contrast, Jesus noted the indifference to him of men who were satisfied with themselves: "They who are whole have no need of a physician." Why would a person who considers himself healthy have any need for strength beyond himself?

The need for God is seldom felt by persons who know

they are very adequate. In a study of "well-adjusted" individuals, the psychologist, A. H. Maslow, found few references to religion. These strong persons had no felt need for salvation from sins, fears, irrational urges. They were persons of good control who led productive lives. They were realistically satisfied with personal accomplishment and contribution to life.

As we defined mental health in chapter 2, these are very healthy people. They have met the highest standards of secular culture.

Holiness and Wholeness

An adequate person does not need health, but he does need holiness. Holiness is a life of awe before the creative power of God. It is an awareness of his majesty, an admission of the gulf between the Creator and his creature.

A holy man is one who knows what God requires of him and depends upon divine strength to accomplish these tasks. "What does the Lord require of you?," asked Micah. The answer is to do justice, love mercy, walk humbly with our God. These requirements transcend mental health. They carry man past psychology into the mysteries of life and death. We leap beyond that which is known into an unknown realm of the spirit. This is faith, an interpretation of men and movements by standards beyond this world.

The "other worldly" emphasis is upon sin and salvation, repentance and grace, humility and long-suffering. Life and death are described as part of a divine order.

The preoccupations of holiness may seem to lead man away from the needs of his world. Indeed, this has happened many times. In chapter 3 we reviewed some specific evidence of church members' indifference to the injustices of their fellowmen.

But preoccupation with the other world is half of holiness. The complete picture includes the needs of our neighbor. As Paul describes this in the second chapter of Ephesians, the grace of Christ does two things for us. First, Christ breaks down the wall of separation between God and man. Second, he reconciles man to man, making them part of a household of faith. They are no longer strangers and sojourners, but fellow citizens with the saints as well as partners in the household of God.

Holiness adds a new dimension to wholeness. Man sees himself and his neighbor in a new light. They are fellow creatures before a heavenly Father. This adds at least two qualities to the existence of man. First, humility in the self. Second, forgiveness of others.

Does this different perspective bring psychological health? It *may,* or it may not. Christ did not promise any kind of health to his disciples. He did promise them some rough times in a hostile world. All they could expect was his spirit to guide and comfort them.

The religion that promises less, produces more. The apostle Paul went through life with a "thorn in the flesh." There were always struggles with himself, as he records in the seventh and eighth chapters of Romans. His writings contain some very narrow views about the rights of women, some hostile jibes at those who oppose him and the open confession that he was often lonely and on the brink of despair.

God changes the directions of a man's life and lets personal characteristics follow. "Growth in grace" is a gradual reshaping of attitudes and actions. Sometimes the rebuilding of a person takes detours. There are chasms where a part of character was neglected or twisted in earlier life. For example, an exploited child becomes a suspicious and extractive adult. These characteristics can be challenged and rechanneled, but who will fill in the love and trust that has been missing for so long? Wise and patient friends or mate can make a big difference. But in times of stress, the old patterns of fear and distrust emerge. It is the better part of mercy to protect such people whenever possible from the reopening of deep wounds. They can make an excellent contribution to life so long as life does not hit them where they have always hurt.

What God Can Do

What good is God if he does not provide complete healing from physical and mental disease?

For many people, the answer is no good. This was the general reaction of a group of mothers who were interviewed during the terminal illness of children with leukemia. When the mothers first heard the diagnosis, many of them prayed. They asked that the diagnosis might be different, that a miracle might be performed, that the life of the child would be spared. After months of treatment, the children were still losing strength. By this time most of the mothers had stopped praying. God did not heal their child, so why should they continue prayer?

Two of the mothers said that prayer meant more to them now than when they first heard the diagnosis. They felt that the companionship of God was most important. Their prayers were for a feeling of his presence. To them, God brought understanding and comfort. Physical health for a child was not the only reason for their religious allegiance.

The experience of these mothers demonstrate religion versus magic. Religion begins in worship, a belief that the favor of God is first. His approval comes before our comfort. Magic puts comfort first. Our desires are primary. We get what we want from some supernatural force by charms, rituals, secret actions. The supernatural powers are supposed to answer our command if we discover their name or hiding place.

The great teachers of every religion have rejected magic. In the Christian Scriptures, God and nature are separated. If a tower falls on a group of people, this does not mean God's displeasure. Specific acts of fortune and good health may be natural occurrences rather than divine intervention. Misfortune and poor health may come to anyone. Jesus healed many persons, but he did not promise health and happiness to his followers. What he did promise was eternal life, beginning now.

Mental health is not a promise of God but it may be

a by-product of faith and fellowship.

Questionnaires and interviews show some relationship between religion and mental health. First, there is the general evidence for happiness and well-being among persons who are regular in church attendance. A study of two thousand Americans showed that marital happiness and job satisfaction increased steadily with reported church attendance.

A questionnaire cannot tell us if religion is contributing to happiness or if happy people feel more comfortable about church attendance. Which influence is greater?

At least we know that regular church attendance is associated more with mental health than it is with illness. Several studies of hospitalized mental patients have shown them to have a lower record of church attendance before hospitalization than is consistent with the general population. A majority of patients in one study showed no particular interest in religion before or during hospitalization.

There are good and bad conclusions from these findings. A good one is that there is no statistical evidence for the assertion that religion makes people crazy. The bad conclusion is that religion seems to be of little help to those in severe emotional crisis. The church may be keeping itself "healthy," but it has little significance for those who are unhealthy.

What Kind of God Is Expected?

Some mental health workers may question these generalizations. They think that some kinds of religion make people sick.

They are right and wrong. They are accurate in seeing some disturbed persons who have been beaten down by legalistic religion. Contempt for self and hate of others can *sound* religious. We may hear on radio broadcast the kind of teaching that some people take with them to a mental clinic or hospital. Before writing this chapter I listened to such a broadcast. A preacher was denouncing the sins of youth. He read lurid stories of a few persons undressing among hundreds of thousands at rock festivals. His conclusion was that the music was responsible for many forms of immorality. His concluding sentence was: "How could anybody listen to *African* music?" People who think like that preacher must exercise rigid control over all their feelings. The outside of the cup must be very, very clean, for the inside filth might seep through. The imagination of these people is really frightening. They have little control over their impulses of hostility and sex. If someone keeps frightening them to be good, they will smother their feelings.

The God of these people is wrathful and vengeful. They must continually appease him by confession of small faults and many good works. To them, a God of love is dangerous. They do not know what to do with warmth and tenderness. It sounds soft and sentimental.

Can we change these peoples' picture of God? Usually we have first to change the picture they have of themselves and others. The dark strivings within an individual must be brought to light. Once he sees that human beings can accept him, he can consider the Christian teaching that God can also accept him.

During the uncovering of forbidden urges, people may become very frightened. They think that talk about "unspeakable" urges is the same as action. In a panic, some refuse any more help. They denounce mental health workers or pastoral counselors as "sex maniacs" or "mother haters." When I was a pastor, one marginal member came to me with a complaint against the local mental hygiene clinic. She said that a counselor told her to commit adultery. When I asked for the specific conversations, she said, "Well, he asked me what I thought about sex, and that's the same as commiting adultery, isn't it?" Since she was a married woman, I asked her if thoughts about sex with her husband should be called evil. She replied, "You're as bad as those psychologists! All men think about is sex. I have my separate bedroom now. But I know my husband is a schemer. The steps to the attic go up through my closet. I know he'll crawl up in the attic through the garage and try to get in my room."

The repressed fears of people like this are preyed upon by rigid religious leaders. Almost every community has heard of some campaign against sex education in public schools. The major point of attack is: "If you give young people information, they'll do something bad." Teachers may protest in vain that the classes include warnings against premarital intercourse. The fearful adult will not listen.

Mental health workers can realistically call that kind

of religion "sick." It is the loveless, rigid emphasis upon rules that was denounced by Jesus and the prophets. But sometimes a professional person will carry the "sick" label too far. He will assume that any mention of judgment or condemnation in religion is wrong.

Mental health workers need some correction at this point. They are making the mistake of judging the religion of others by their own cultural standards. Since most professional workers are college graduates, they tend to accept the assumptions of the established denominations, Episcopalian, Presbyterian, United Church of Christ. These are the denominations with the highest percentage of college graduates. In these denominations, and in the Baptist and Methodist churches near universities, there would be a positive attitude toward God as a loving heavenly Father. He is personally concerned about the welfare of all his children. To be religious is to be concerned about the welfare of others. We show this concern by "unconditional acceptance." These are the assumptions that a chaplain and a psychologist found in a study of persons in Sunday School classes in Atlanta, Georgia. In contrast, they found that many patients in a state mental hospital had a different view of God. The patients saw God as a very personal being. He was not as theoretical as he was to the college graduates. Furthermore, God could get angry, just like a father who cared for his children. He would punish those who disobeyed his rules. The patients had a grade school or high school education. This accounted for the difference in their views of God.

When this report was made to some professional people, they admitted that they disliked "punitive" religion, but they recognized that this was the religion of many people who came from a different part of the city. Since they only saw those people in mental health clinics, they often assumed that the sickness of the person and the religion that he expressed were one. Actually, they were hearing about religious beliefs accepted by healthy as well as unhealthy people who had a grade school or high school education. Poorly educated patients were more literal in their beliefs about God, but this did not mean that their religion was sick.

How can these cultural confusions be reduced? Some mental health clinics have solved this by regular meetings of some of their staff with clergymen and other professionals in the community. One month a case is presented by the staff, the next month a case is presented from the community.

On one occasion a pastor described a woman's ideas about the church and her marriage. She was suspicious of her husband and thought that God had condemned most of the hypocrites who sat in church with her. The pastor described three years of occasional meetings with the woman and her husband. She had much respect for the pastor as ultimate authority. When he told her not to judge the people in the church and to show more affection for her husband, she began to modify her attitudes. Still, after three years she cannot "get along" with many members of the congregation and is not as loving as her husband desires. The minister wondered what more he could do. "What more could you do!" said a psychologist. "I wish I had the patience to stay with that kind of counseling relationship for three years. You've done a great job." By professional standards, the minister had made much progress with a difficult case. But he had judged himself by idealistic religious standards, and thought he was a failure.

On another occasion, a social worker who had recently come to the community from another section of the country described a laborer who had "delusions." She was puzzled because his behavior seemed to be normal. But she had interviewed him when his child was being tested in a school clinic. He asked the worker if she were "saved." When she asked what that meant, he told her about "salvation through the blood." He spoke of the joy of his own religion. "Why," he said, "I can sit in my room and just imagine Jesus on the cross dying for me." The social worker was alarmed by these references to blood and suffering. She wanted to know what this meant. When a minister explained that this was the "garden variety" religion of the region, she was relieved. She said, "I could not understand how such a kind, passive person could have had such blood-thirsty thoughts."

When Does God Make a Difference?

Jesus told his disciples that they did not receive much from God because they did not know how to ask. We must know what to ask for and when to ask for it.

When does God make a difference? Adults who made a profession of faith in Texas Presbyterian churches were asked this question. They usually mentioned a move to a new city, a change of jobs, marriage, the birth of a child, the time when a child joined the church.

These are occasions when the picture of ourself is being challenged. Can we make good in a new position? Are we adequate as spouse or parent? These are times that shake our confidence. When our strength is small, we think of power beyond ourselves.

Professions during these crucial experiences of life are enduring. They are based on the biblical understanding of God's nature. He has made man for communion with him. Man is to recognize that he is a creature and that strength beyond himself is needed for growth and maturity.

These professions are different from the cry of someone who is in a jam. Many of those persons give up their religion as soon as the crisis is passed.

The adults who made a profession were more concerned about God's opinion of them than they were about some favor they would receive. Their typical comment was that conversion meant a closer relationship to God, a sense of acceptance by him, a forgiveness of sin, a belief that things were now right for them. The psychologist who did this study called these answers a "mystical" factor. They described a general relationship to the diety. There was no specific occasion or personal request which would identify a request *from* God.

God makes a difference during the trying experiences that open our eyes to human inadequacy. He can provide strength and assurance that our eternal commitments are secure, no matter what may happen in the turmoil of life.

When the trials of life are too much for a person, they may then turn toward a savior. The way in which they turn makes quite a difference. Those who look for quick and easy results are dissatisfied. Those who seek an enduring relationship are satisfied. They find that God has some answers for those who will accept a new quality of life.

A key to this quality of life is personal responsibility for suffering. This has often been observed by the chaplains who work with mental patients. One patient conceals his failures. Another projects blame on others. But some people in trouble can be honest. With support and guidance they can see themselves and others as they really are. Steadily they move to an understanding of why they are in such a mess.

The recalling of past experiences is painful. The admission of personal responsibility for some mistakes is humiliating. It is difficult to give up general accusations and specify specific hurts. One minister in a hospital had to admit that his condemnation of all his church leaders was in error. There was some specific men who hated him and he hated them. They were in a power struggle and he had lost. He came to the hospital because he could not sleep. He paced the floor each night with a rage that he could not admit.

When the man admitted how he had been hurt, he then

faced a new problem. Could he forgive those who dominated him? This question was only partially answered by the time he returned to his pastorate. What he did say on leaving was this: "Well, at least I will not pretend that I am invulnerable to what they say and do. I'll have to be honest about my own feelings. I'll also have to admit some of my own mistakes openly. There are some people who care about me in that congregation, and I guess they go through some of the same struggles that I do. Maybe we can build a church together."

God can make a difference in mental health. Honesty, humility, responsibility are moral qualities that are connected to Christian living and psychological well being.

There is a need for caution, however. The essential goal of religion is salvation. It may be found by a person who still has psychological inadequacies. It may take much cooperation between church and clinic for him to participate in human as well as divine experiences of love.

We must also remember that a person can be psychologically adequate and spiritually dead.

CHAPTER VI
IS SIN REAL?

The aim of mental health is to make a neurotic sinner into a healthy one. Psychotherapy seeks functional wholeness, not holiness.

In a mental health clinic, the battle is not between sin and salvation. It is a fight for commitment to human emotion among people who don't know how they feel, or who despair at the possibility of any satisfying feelings.

The fight for feeling goes in and out. Inwardly, there is the problem of repressed emotion from the past. A person may be chronically despondent because of tragedies in early life. Constant bickering at home might have led the person as a child to assume that he was no good and live among people who only hurt one another. A patient who lived through this told me: "I saw my father beat my mother, but I was too small to help her. I saw, but I didn't see. I mean, I looked, but I kept my thoughts to myself. He might have killed me." It is no wonder that this man was shy and moody as an adult. He had been trained for years to bottle up hatred in himself.

The understanding of these secrets from the past is one part of therapy. Another part moves out of the self toward others. Our present relationships have much to do with our feeling or the lack of it. The patient who "saw but did not see" came to a hospital because of a recent tragedy in his marriage. His wife was unfaithful. He could not be angry with her, for he had never talked back to anyone. All he could do was leave the house. He withdrew now as he had from his father years before.

Gradually the man was able to tell how he hurt now. I helped connect his present reactions to his lifetime pattern of withdrawal. Maybe he would never be able to tell some people what he thought of them, but at least he could openly admit to himself what was happening. Perhaps he could tell someone like me. That would be safe and acceptable.

The search for feeling is a longing for love. A young man who had been on drugs said this: "I never could shoot straight about myself until I came here. Then I saw that people would accept me if I told how I really felt. When I could do some confessing, I really felt that someone loved me. They listened and they cared. That's never happened to me before."

The young man was helped because he decided to be

himself. Honesty was worth the risk. But many other persons cannot make a decision. They are in and out of "inquiry groups." These are groups established for young people on drugs who must decide to "kick" the habit if they are to come everyday for conversations with others who have been addicted. When a person is "clean" for a period of time, he may then be enrolled as the regular member of a therapy group, or be admitted to a hospital for treatment.

Successful treatment requires an act of the will as well as an acceptance of love. Therapists are fighting apathy and indecision. The client must make some commitment, take some risk if he is to be helped. If he wants to be a different person he must have some courage to move in a different direction. As a theologian, Paul Tillich, put it, he must have the "courage to be."

What's in a Name?

In a best seller, *Love and Will,* Dr. Rollo May has written that men get better when they are willing to face the force of evil in themselves and the world. They are helped in this by professional people who give names to evil.

Psychologically, evil may be defined as the rising up of one part of the self over the whole person. Sex, anger, or power may be distorted in this way to destroy personality.

What shall we call these forces of destruction? The doctor gives the label of illness. Rollo May writes: "Diagnosis may be considered our modern form of naming the offending demon." [1] The patient is strengthened by this labeling. The name is a symbol for the attitude that he and the therapist will take toward the disorder in his life. The unknown has become manageable.

Would psychological forces of destruction be changed by another name? Would it make any difference if we talked about sin rather than sickness?

A different name means a different outlook. This was well understood by the Hebrews, who recognized the significance of identification. When Jacob wrestled with an angel before the coming of the brother that he feared, some change took place in his life. This is labeled by the angelic being who fought him. Jacob will have a new name, Israel.

Jesus and his disciples followed the same emphasis. Simon becomes Peter after a confession of faith. Saul is named Paul after his conversion. A new direction in life is signified by a change of name.

The labels that we give to psychological forces are guides to our direction in life. When psychoanalysts relate guilt feelings to "Oedipul conflicts," they are emphasizing the early relationship between parent and child. That relationship triangle is the base upon which they would reconstruct a personality. Other analysts, like Erik Erickson, stress identity and anxiety, shame and guilt. They focus as much attention upon present relationships as upon the primary impressions of childhood. A strong emphasis upon the future would be found in the writings of Viktor Frankl. In his "logotherapy," clients are challenged to look beyond themselves as a way of solving the conflicts within themselves.

The labels of each theory point the direction: backward, inward, outward, forward. Upward is the only direction missing. This direction is signaled by "sin," "salvation," "repentance," "forgiveness." These are God-ward words.

Sin describes a different dimension of human existence. It is a description of man's relation to God. It is an ultimate concern. "For what purpose do I live?" is the essential question of mankind. The religious answer is, "We live for God despite the threat of death, sin, meaninglessness."

"Ultimate concern" sounds vague to many mental health professionals. They have been trained to identify and deal with human emotions. When we talk about indecision or lack of feeling they can visualize the struggles of a specific patient. They can relate a conversation about loneliness and guilt to personal experience.

Talk about God, sin, the devil, seems too far beyond their personal or professional interest. They have been taught tolerance of a person's religious belief, but they wonder how anyone connects God to human experience in a healthy way.

The concept of sin is not only vague to many professionals, but it often interferes with their service to people. A social worker may be confronted by an angry mother who says: "I'll not bring my child to this clinic again. It's full of sin. I heard some workers in the hall use language that I would never repeat. And the woman who talks to my child was smoking a cigarette in her office when we walked by."

The social worker will label this "legalism," "rigidity," "defensiveness." She's right. But she might make a mistake and relate all conversation about sin to rigid and defensive thinking.

It is easy to assume in a clinic that a sense of sin is unhealthy. There are several reasons for this. First, there are many conversations like the one of an angry mother with the social worker. People pretend self-righteousness as a means of escape from hard truths about their relationships with other people. A person who is blind to his own conceit will often sound righteous. After many interviews with one patient, the time came for some honest confrontation. I asked the patient: "You have spoken many times of your desire to do God's will. As I think of God's will, the love of man is a primary command. You will have difficulty with that command. You often tell me of difficulties in living with other patients. How could you learn to care for them?"

The patient opened his eyes wide and said: "But God does not want me to love *those* people; they are sinners. They play cards all day on the ward. They curse and smoke. I would compromise with sin to care for them."

Confronted by that kind of dissent, most professionals would avoid any conversation about "sin" and center the discussion on the patient's feelings about himself and his fellow men. They don't see how anyone would be helped by more legalistic labels.

Professionals are especially incensed by the use of legalism for self-destruction. They meet many persons who carry staggering loads of self-imposed guilt. This is the second reason why mental health workers wonder if sin is real. In clinics it is so often connected with pathological feelings of unworthiness. The worker wants people to feel *more* worthy. Clients who talk about their sins may be suffering from an overdeveloped conscience. This used to be called scrupulosity. Now we call it neurosis.

The resolution of conflicts of conscience usually explains sin away. For example, I talked as a pastor with the mother of five children who was expecting a sixth. She thought an unpardonable sin had been committed because she wished for an abortion. Several conversations revealed her as a conscientious person who was trying to manage the household with no help from her husband. She was unwilling to express her resentment against him and felt very guilty for her exasperation with the children. With some encouragement from me she gradually learned to bring her husband into family decisions. When he began to act more like a father, she was happier as a mother. They made plans together for another child.

When Is a Sinner a Saint?

Legalism and a sense of unworthiness are often the ways in which mental health workers hear about "sin." This is enough to inhibit their discussion of the subject.

But when you are trying to help people, you must give some attention to their way of looking at life. So, clients are encouraged to relate their system of values to the ethical standards, customs and practices of the community in which they live.

But here again, the worker gets a poor picture of "sin." Many persons connect cultural practices with the very commands of God. To disobey a custom is to commit sin. This was one of the original problems for psychoanalytic treatment. Well-bred women in nineteenth-century Vienna had been taught to inhibit sexual feelings. When they began to experience pleasure in marriage, or to wish for it, the thoughts were terrifying. The feelings were repressed and emerged later as hysteria. Freud and his followers fought against a culture that created such conflicts.

Their fight has been so successful in middle-class America that the fig leaf has now fluttered up to cover the face. That is, people are very reluctant to reveal much about themselves, their beliefs, their inner strivings, but they are quite relaxed about sexual exposure. A "sophisticated" person may talk about or look at a sexual activity, and yet be very shy in expressing his hopes and fears, beliefs and doubts.

Culture changes the definition of sins. The moral standards of Victorian ancestors are now considered unhealthy in upper middle-class America. Conversely, the confession of sin and the expression of religious feeling, which was typical of American Protestants in the nineteenth century, is now an uncomfortable subject.

With so many shifts in custom, how can anyone identify sin? The sinners of one generation seem like saints in another. The accepted practices in one culture are forbidden in another part of the world. When feelings of guilt are so relative, how can anyone talk about permanent standards or ultimate concern?

Punishment and Forgiveness

Jesus and the prophets had the same objections as mental health workers to the way that people talk about sin. Early Christianity cut the connection between culture and faith. The apostle Paul wrote that neither the observance of Jewish nor any other customs would fulfil righteousness. A man of faith was not to be burdened with questions about "touch not, taste not," or other regulations. He was to love his neighbor, whether the neighbor was "clean" or "unclean."

The Bible is full of attacks upon self-righteousness as a defense. Jesus accused religious leaders of his day as blind leaders of the blind. They laid heavy burdens of regulations upon others, and could not see their conceit.

Legalism, self-conceit, conformity to custom are condemned in the Prophets, the Gospels, and the Epistles. Yet all of these writings emphasize sin. There must be some distinctions that can be noted. What is "sin" in the religious sense of the word?

Sin is offense against God. It is an unwillingness to live as a creature with limitations who must depend upon the power of a creator.

Sin begins in anxiety. Instead of an acceptance of finiteness, men become more or less than they were intended to be. "More than" means pride. "Less than" means sensuality. Paul gives a succinct description of this dilemma in the first chapter of his letter to the Romans.

Anxiety, pride, and sensuality are very human terms. They have natural consequences which we call guilt. Guilt includes a fear of punishment. This may come from the self or other people. It may include feelings about God as an angry father who will hurt those who do not obey him.

When we correct a person's relationship to God, we transform feelings of guilt into sin. Instead of a fear of punishment, a person feels ashamed that he has outraged God's love. He is not so concerned about violations as he is about relationships.

Guilt means regret; sin leads to repentance. Regret is taken away when the guilty person is assured that an injury has been repaired and that he will suffer no harm. Sin is cleansed when a person feels he is accepted by God despite his waywardness.

There is an equality of all men when we talk about sin. All fall short of the glory of God. It is an all encompassing term for our human condition. An awareness of this condition leads to humility before God and service to men. Sin is a sense of inability to be all that God desires. An acceptance of this state and submission to the Creator gives courage to live out an incomplete life with hope and charity.

Sin enters psychotherapy in two ways. First, there is the general sense of which we have just spoken. Men gain balance and perspective in life when they know their limitations and accept an anchor beyond themselves. This is often an elusive goal. But the question must be faced: "When are you going to stop living above your psychological means?" The self-made man, who has always done his best by his own strength, must eventually come to terms with his need to depend upon others.

Or we may ask a person: "Why are you pretending to be less than human?" A woman may have dissolved herself in "motherhood." She devotes her life to the children in such a way that there is no time for her own interests or for creative activity with her husband and friends. Now, the children are leaving home and she is vaguely depressed. Why? Because she would not think of herself as a human being with individual needs and desires. She buried herself and now feels dead.

The theological remedy for this condition is called "the image of God." Women as well as men are to be individuals. They cannot fulfil God's purpose in their life without an awareness of who they are and what they can do.

The prescription for the woman is often different than it is for the man. Women fall short of God's demands by denying individuality. Men offend God by pride in their personal accomplishments.

These generalizations may sound vague, and they can be contradicted by individual cases. The big statements are made because we are dealing with a basic problem, the meaning of life.

We can be more specific about a second function of sin in psychotherapy. This is the important area of conviction, confession, repentance, restitution. A minister is often called for in a mental health clinic when a person has been brought to this stage of religious experience.

Sometime the clergyman serves as a consultant to another professional who is seeing the client. A mental health worker will often see the need to explore attitudes and actions that have religious overtones, but he wants to be sure that religious traditions are not offended or a theological issue misidentified.

A social worker asked a minister if the abstinence of sexual relations were a penance imposed in his church. When the clergyman said no, the social worker discussed the current case of a devout woman who had accidentally injured a child in an automobile wreck. The woman was first distraught and then sank into a depression. As she began to recover from her moods, she vowed a holy life to God. One part of this vow was the demand for a separate bedroom. The social worker wanted to explore this vow in more detail. Was the woman seeking to punish herself or her husband? Was this a sign of deep seated sexual disturbance or some misguided part of a religious tradition?

Clergyman and other mental health professionals can often be in consultation about the blending of theological, psychological, social, and cultural factors in healing. In addition, there will be specific instances when a religious authority must be counselor rather than consultant. This often occurs when a person cannot achieve forgiveness. The usual task of the minister is to separate the complete forgiveness of God from the incomplete forgiveness of ourselves and others.

A young husband sought the help of a mental health worker to "make my wife happy again." He explained that they had been in love for four years and had delayed marriage until he finished college. But the strain of waiting had proved too great and she had become pregnant during one of the intense weekends they spent at the end of his semester of study. They married immediately after she knew her condition and were very happy until the birth of the child. Then his mother-in-law said "I have never known such shame in my life. People are asking how a nine pound baby can be born seven months after marriage. When I sing in the church choir, I think of all the things that people are saying about me. How could you do this to your mother?" This was repeated on weekly occasions in family gatherings.

The young wife was persuaded to visit the clinic. The couple talked together with a psychologist about their marriage relationship, their love for the child, their double-minded feelings about the mother-in-law. From time to time the young woman would say, "But I cannot forgive myself."

When she was asked if she were willing to talk with her minister, she said, "Yes." In three visits, the pastor sought to separate the steadfast love of God from the selfish love of a mother. God was capable of complete forgiveness. The mother, anxious for social status and security, could not attain this. Could the young woman accept the imperfection of her mother and be satisfied with the perfect acceptance she could receive from God? If she were willing to accept the power of God's healing, she might be less concerned about approval from a powerful mother.

The conversations also dealt with the same theme in her own consciousness. Could she accept her own limitations and confess to God that she had failed? He was certainly willing to receive her confession, but was she willing to admit that she could make a real mistake with painful social consequences? From her mother she had received an idealized picture of herself. Now it was broken. Would she be willing to lead a happy life as an incomplete person?

There was no complete resolution of the problems in this young lady's life. But a sustaining force was introduced. She not only gained psychological understanding. She also began to realize the reality of a power beyond mother or the ideal picture she had of herself. When God becomes real, sin can be forgiven.

NOTES
1. *Psychology Today,* August, 1969, p. 47.

CHAPTER VII
DO WE STILL NEED PASTORS?

The cure of sickness comes before the care of souls in modern society. The preoccupation of middle-class Americans is success and security in this life. Those who contribute to today's happiness are highly regarded.

What place does a clergyman have in such a society? Can he really help people? Is his ministry irrelevant to the concerns of modern man?

These questions challenge the church in two ways. First, we are in days of rapid change when established values are being shaken. The assumptions of theology and the value of the church in society are no longer taken for granted. We must provide thoughtful answers to these searching queries.

Second, the church must compete with other professions for the allegiance of young men and women who want to help people. Many young people feel that they will have more freedom of thought, financial security, and resources for service in the field of mental health, the Office of Economic Opportunity, a comprehensive health care center, or a Head Start program. Each of these programs are built on the premise that people in distress should be helped. The money and power that go with these positions are great in comparison with the voluntary contributions of churchmen to any program for the sick or poor.

As a result of this challenge, the church must fight a continuing battle to recruit and maintain professional leadership. There are aggressive campaigns in community colleges and in state universities for young people who want to help others. A high school graduate may be recruited for a two-year program in a community college that will lead to an associate of arts degree in mental health. He or she will spend part time in a mental health clinic or hospital as part of the experience toward a degree. From the first day of college, a student is presented with attractive opportunities for service to others.

Community colleges and mental health centers grow together. The first provides courses that train the manpower for the second. The mental health center demonstrates the relevance of the training provided in the community college. Since the growth of community colleges is now akin to the growth of high schools in a previous generation, we can realize the impact of these institutions upon the young people of the present generation.

The time has passed when godly parents could safely assume that a religious youth would enter a church vocation. When the youth could choose only between public-school teaching and the ministry, the supply of ministers was secure. But that world disappeared in World War II.

One comforting answer to this challenge is to say: "If God calls a man, he will surely enter the ministry." Unfortunately for those who find security in this slogan, the application has changed. We used to think that a divine call meant preaching. Now we find many people interpreting the call of God to mean any service to others in his name.

This is the interpretation given by four hundred former ministers of the United Church of Christ. Most of these men had served for ten years in the pastorate after graduation from a theological seminary. They were not only experienced pastors, but they also were better educated than the average minister in their denomination. A significant number had graduate degrees.

When these men were asked about their present position in other professions, they replied that they were still in the ministry, but they were not actively employed by the church. As they see it, work as a teacher, counselor, or social worker is an authentic ministry of Christ. They see no reason why the call of God should be restricted to preaching from a pulpit on Sunday morning or to pay from an ecclesiastical organization.

With the expression of these opinions from experienced

clergymen, churches can no longer assume that a divine call will put a man in the pulpit. The sense of divine mission that led men of one generation into the church may lead men of the present generation into other professions.

We may argue that the interpretation of the call is now so broad that it has lost specific meaning. But our problem is with alert young people who have this broad interpretation. Can we still attract them to a church vocation?

One problem is the recruitment of qualified young people for church vocations. Another problem is their training. The men who go to denominational seminaries are usually interested in a pastoral ministry. About 90 percent of the Presbyterian and Baptist students go directly into the pastorate, according to recent surveys. The 10 percent who go into related professions deserve some attention. Psychological tests show many of them to be creative and aggressive people. They could make a contribution to churches that need some change. But they are attracted by other professions that offer immediate sources for healing. They like a place where their imagination is appreciated and used.

If we wish *safe* change, we will not worry much about that 10 percent. A section of the country can insulate itself with ministers who think carefully and slowly. But the national trends are out of local control. The intellectual leadership for most denominations will come from interdenominational seminaries. The presidents of these seminaries report that less than half of their graduates are seeking pastorates. They are not interested in traditional ministries. What will the church do to encourage these intelligent and irritating young people toward leadership for the future?

The answer of some denominations has been apathy. As a result, mental health and other fields are enriched with talent that might have served the institutional church. State personnel directors are happy to find graduates of seminaries and experienced ministers who serve competently as chaplains, vocational counselors, social workers, drug and alcohol counselors, directors of mental health centers. Ministers are excellent in these fields. They are already motivated to help people and their training has given them a broad philosophical background for any additional training they need in in a particular type of therapy.

The mental health movement is gaining manpower from churches, while many churches discourage sensitive pastors who remain. A nationwide study of Presbyterian ministers reveals their frustration with the selfishness of congregations. The ministers knew that Christian faith required care for others, but they could not turn their people toward the world. Instead, they found the principle objection to charity in their own leadership. Leaders counseled more attention to the local church program and the exclusion of social issues.

It is heartbreaking to preach God's love for the world to people who only love themselves. We may ask, Why do men who care for people stay in the pastorate?

The Same Old Story

Men remain in the pastorate because they have a story to tell. It is the unfolding drama of God's love for the world. The fascinating story of Jesus is the central delight of a Christian minister. In one denomination it will be expressed through preaching and personal evangelism. In another it is dramatized through public and private sacraments. Whatever the method, the message is the same: eternal life is available now through faith in Christ.

This is an old story. Men retell it because they need to establish the theological basis for life. The world does not make much sense as it is. The Christian message tries to make sense out of our nonsense.

The story makes sense to those who look beyond the senses. This is faith, an interpretation of that which is seen in the light of that which is unseen. The life of man is to be ordered by a mysterious force that cannot be scientifically demonstrated.

This supernaturalism is the Christian answer to life and death. It is the triumph of a spiritual force over sin, hell, and the grave. Supernaturalism is a stumbling block to some ministers. The language and thought of theology seems irrelevant. Irrelevant to what? Here we come to an assumption of faith. One man believes that life and death can be explained or endured in terms of interpersonal relationships. He believes in that which he can feel. Another is dissatisfied with such an interpretation. He looks beyond that which can be seen to that which is unseen.

One philosophy of life is as logical as the other. The basic question is, do we put our trust in God or in man?

I do not make this distinction in order to cut the love of God from the love of neighbor. The two are one. But there is a qualitative difference between God and neighbor. One is the Creator and the other is a fellow creature. It is this recognition that separates spiritual religion from ethical humanism.

We need pastors because men must find God. The great commission of a minister is to tell and live the message that will compel men to come into God's kingdom.

Many professions may lead men toward God, but only one has this central mission. Without this message, the ministry is really irrelevant. If a clergymen does not relate men to God, what is his professional purpose?

The Measured Life

The first purpose of a pastor is to tell men what to live for. His second purpose is to tell them how to live.

The "how" is growth in grace. It is the development of character. We measure this character by the personal virtues that have been described in an earlier chapter.

Ministers measure virtue. They present a standard for life. As we have already seen, expectations must be related to personal growth and social expectations. Moral requirements must fit developmental tasks.

In preaching and practice, the clergyman represents standards of virtue. This is completely unacceptable to some ministers who have received the poor counsel of hypocrisy. They have been taught that conformity to the customs of a region would win approval. This was equated with virtue. It is no wonder that ministers and many other professionals react to "standards," "values," and "virtues" because of their associations with manners that please powerful men and make circumstances easy.

Despite these unfavorable associations, an essential function of the ministry is character molding. People identify with a man or woman who shows the quality of life that Jesus demonstrated with his disciples.

The tragedy of the ministry is that many men have not known or are not permitted to present the central virtues of the faith. They should lead people toward faith, hope, charity, forgiveness, courage, mercy and wisdom. These are the great goals of healing for any profession.

But the minister and his wife have often been regarded as little more than clotheshorses for a culture. They parade the accepted customs of a region. The minister and his wife are to dress in a certain way, associate with a certain crowd of church leaders, keep their children from unacceptable places, and avoid controversial subjects. The result is a caricature that has been mercilessly portrayed in modern secular literature.

The minister who stands against this caricature will threaten conformists in his congregation. But he will be free for an essential ministry. He can teach and practice the cardinal virtues.

There is no greater natural task for man. A psychiatric resident once complained to me: "I have learned how to reduce anxiety and explain the unexpressed fears of Mrs. (a patient). Now my supervisor says that she must accept responsibility for her children and the happiness of her husband. He also wants me to get her involved in the church or some community activity. But how can I do that? That requires maturity. This woman is a child. How do you teach someone maturity?

Maturity is the goal of mental health. In Christian faith it is one of the "fruits of the spirit." Many counselors aid people toward maturity. The special function of a clergyman is to measure growth in spiritual terms. He defines the relationship of a man to himself and to his neighbor by the stature of Christ. His measurement is humility, sacrifice, concern for others.

These are high standards. But this is what we expect of religion. It defines which is highest and best for man. The goals are beyond our natural abilities. Supernatural grace is required for perfection.

Words like grace and perfection sound stiff and stupid to many sensitive people. They have seen the misapplication of virtue. There are religious leaders who compulsively identify the behavior of a thirteen-year-old boy with the thoughts of a forty-five-year-old man. There are women of the church who believe that a sweet smile and soft words can smother any evil or hostility, even their own.

Our problem is not with the standards, but with their application. Virtue without prudence is vice. The first requirement of ethics is reality. We must judge the situation accurately and understand the persons who are involved. Only then will we know the proper measure for a man's life.

A minister is required to be more than faithful in the preaching and practice of ethics. He must also be wise in the application of these values. His first virtue is prudence. As Jesus warned those who heard him by the Sea of Galilee, the measure you have for others is the one with which you will be measured.

How will a pastor be prepared for the right exercise of judgment? Two requirements have come out of the American religious tradition. One is a personal experience of God's grace. The clergyman is expected to be a converted man. He should be able to testify of that which has occurred in his own life.

This is one way to meet the requirement that Jesus stated in the fifth chapter of Matthew. A man must first accept God's judgment upon his own life before he can presume to guide others. The beam must be removed from his own eye before he can see clearly the mote in another.

The second requirement is training in a biblical tradition. This will include theology and the expectations of the denomination to which he belongs. He will have a specific area of specialization, the knowledge of God as revealed to man.

A third requirement is now being added to the traditional ones. It is the demand for expertness in the religious consciousness. A pastor is expected to know how God works in the hearts of men. He is a physician of the soul who can recognize religious elements in psychological states of being. He is a shepherd who guides the mind by spiritual principles.

This third requirement is not a new one in the history of pastoral care, but it has new significance in the last half of the twentieth century. The developments in mental health have made the public aware of the inner world of man.

Rocking the Ark

The Christian religion requires two directions for man. One is "upward" or "inward." It is the awareness of God's presence in our lives. The other is "outward," the requirement to love our neighbor as ourselves.

These requirements of faith are inseparable. The true mystic always becomes a prophet. As Isaiah recorded his classic religious experience, he was first filled with awe before God, and then heard a voice sending him forth to the people.

The lay leadership of most American churches have sought to exalt the mystic and repress the prophet. One of the great tasks of a modern minister is to reject this separation and strengthen the work of the church in the world.

A prophetic ministry will rock the ark. The church has been such a refuge for people who could not face the moral requirements of a new generation. Despite the courageous efforts of a minority, a majority of lay leaders have fought every attempt to involve the church in justice for poor and oppressed people. One justification for this has been an exclusive emphasis upon the mystical or evangelistic side of Christianity. Another has been the pragmatic statement that people will be insecure and angry. They will stop giving or coming to church. Then the new buildings will be half filled and unpaid for.

There are always a few people who oppose this selfishness. The exciting task of a pastor is to transform this minority into a majority. He must lead most of the people beyond the superficial security of a private religious experience into the disturbing world of social service and action.

To turn a church "inside out," a minister needs knowledge of both God and man. On the one hand he must continually relate the challenge of Christian faith to the requirements of modern society. On the other hand, he must understand personal motivation and group processes. This is required both in his leadership of the church and his relationships in the community.

Most ministers confess their inadequacies when confronted with these requirements. Few of them have received the necessary training in psychology of religion, group leadership, and social systems. Some of this need can be supplied through alliances with mental health professionals and others who have training and experience in community development.

At the same time, the minister has resources which are not bestowed upon other community leaders. He has been "set apart" by the church to tell people what God requires of them. He is a judge of right and wrong. His statements relate current social problems to the endurinig tradition of a religious group.

This is a powerful resource for social change. It combines religious motivation with social awareness. It provides the stability of an enduring tradition while adjustments are made in the current culture. It gives individuals the strength of a group who share their enduring ideals.

Wisdom and humility are the necessary virtues that guide the use of these theological resources. Wisdom is needed for timing and application. What is the real situation and what contribution can Christian people make? There are many compromises and delays in the changing of social order. How can courage and action be united with patience and statesmanship?

The answers to these questions require a spirit of humility. A minister is to be certain about some things. The temptation is to be certain about too much. He will need the guidance of experts in other fields for many decisions. The counsel of laymen will be necessary for group support in the church. More experienced and trained leaders in the community may give the best advice, while he follows.

If the minister has the virtues of prudence and humility, he can add the enduring quality of religious justice and mercy to movements for social reform. He represents a tradition of mercy and forgiveness that transcends the prejudices of a culture. His fight for the education of mentally retarded children, the care of unwed mothers, the rehabilitation of alcoholics, or the social acceptance of persons who have been mentally ill is an expected part of his two-thousand year heritage. He can speak to the "establishment" when newer professions might be dismissed as "new fangled government programs." Above all, he can rekindle the association of his congregation with their prophetic heritage. He can call pilgrims out of the ark into the world.

The Pastor in a New World

The church needs pastors who will know God and the world. But if a pastor has an interest beyond the bounds of institutional religion, what will the world think of him?

The world of mental health is looking for specialists in psychology of religion. A pastor is the professional person to whom we refer many questions on the meaning of life, the tragedy of death, grief, sin, and the spirit of forgiveness. There are some complicated problems about the religious consciousness that require consultation with ministers. Is a patient expressing a heightened awareness of God or masking an unhealthy mind behind spiritual terms? What are the mature goals of life that may be required of a person? When should a patient be made anxious about a way of life that is morally destructive?

Community mental health clinics need the active support and consultation of ministers who enjoy these questions. I say "enjoy" because they should be the center of the ministers thought and training. If this is so, he is the most competent person for consultation with staff or conversations with clients. Some clinics employ ministers on a part- or full-time basis to perform this function. The advantage of this relationship is the integration of religion with other thoughts about the problems of people. The disadvantage is a minister's temptation to become more scientific than religious. He may be impressed with the learning of a psychiatrist, the observations of a psychologist, the skill of a social worker or nurse. His desire to be like them may be stronger than his willingness to contribute theological understanding. Soon he may speak the language of mental health and make superficial comparisons between the diagnostic terms of illness and the spiritual concepts of faith.

The local pastor is less often tempted than the chaplain to disguise or blur his role. He may not be as close to the thinking and action of a clinic, but he has much that the clinic needs in his position. He can provide information about the history of a patient and family that is often unavailable through interviews or testing. He is often the gatekeeper, who recommends that a troubled person go to a mental health professional. It is his faith and assurance that opens the door to a trusting relationship.

A pastor is often the person who can see that fathers or husbands attend family therapy. He can be aggressive in going to homes and offices for visits. There is a freedom and mobility in his contacts with people that is the envy of other professions.

The pastor is often the interpreter of mental health procedures to resistant family members or anxious relatives. If he approves of what is being done, he can explain the value to fearful people who trust his traditional role but not that of a new counselor.

A minister is often the key to social acceptance of persons who have been disturbed in the past but are now convalescing. He is a protector of children who are at the mercy of cruel persons in the community. Most of those who taunt the families of the mentally ill are cowardly. A strong word from a respected religious authority is usually enough to shut their mouths.

Beyond help to individuals there is the more general task of education. The minister who supports discussions by mental health workers on prevention and rehabilitation will help to give sanction and permanence to a new agency. He is also the one who is often consulted by people who want to help in this new field, but do not know what they can do. One of the pastor's joys is to recommend an activity for a committed person and then see the fulfilment that this activity brings to the volunteer worker and the service that he renders to those in need.

CHAPTER VIII
WHAT CAN I DO?

Every layman should be a minister and the minister should be a coach. This was the motto of two hundred business and professional men in Louisville, Kentucky. As representatives of major Protestant denominations, they met monthly with public and institutional officials to serve hospitals, prisons, and child care institutions in the name of Christ. They were in church on Sunday, but they took the church into the forgotten corners of the community during the week. Through their efforts, a chaplaincy program was established in a large state mental hospital. With the chaplains guidance, churches organized monthly parties for two thousand patients on fifteen wards. At Christmas, they cooperated with a local broadcaster to find a package for each of six hundred patients who had no contact in a year with their families. When the legislature met, they took the lead in a movement to double the appropriations for mental health in the state.

Could the people of other churches in other states do the same?

As a Citizen

The front line responsibility of Christians is as citizens who can sell a new idea, bring people together, open doors in the community, maintain helping programs.

A group of church women felt the impelling force of a new program for their community through a nurse who worked with the local health department. This woman told others of the hundreds of thousands of dollars that would be available in the next few years for their city through the mental health legislation that began in 1963. When the women first talked to city officials, they were told that there was no need for an expanded mental health program. Furthermore, taxpayers would not want the additional burden of a costly program after federal funds had been expended over an eight-year-period.

Several of the women served their church as volunteers in a rehabilitation center. They took the lead in writing a variety of public officials and board members of public agencies to encourage the development of new health services. One official remarked later that he had never received so many handwritten letters from the wives of affluent leaders in the community.

The letters were followed up by personal visits to political leaders. As the result of this interest, the health department was directed to begin planning for community mental health centers. Before the planning was complete, there was a new election year and different officials took office. The women began their work over again with a new party. This time they pressed for a specific request for funds. There were exasperating delays. Boards that were to pass on plans would not meet for months. Officials could not imagine why anyone would want to spend money on these new programs. With each delay, the women increased their range of concern, from individuals to community meetings, to newspapers, radio, and television. Finally, when appropriations for a community mental health center became front page news, official action was taken to accept federal funds for a center.

Several of the women said that there were two sources of strength during the years of delay and indecision. One was their personal contact with people in need through the rehabilitation center. They could see people who needed help. Second, there was the fellowship of their church circles. Here they met for prayer and inspiration.

The women had sold a new idea. But that is only the first job of a citizen. A second step is the ministry of reconciliation. The new and the old must be brought together. Established programs must make way for untried organizations.

The elder of a Presbyterian church described this binding together: "I was chairman of the board of this new agency that brought all the existing programs together.

We had to tell some people that unless they came to the meeting, we would plan their budget for them next year. So they all sat down together.

"Then we had to fight between professions. Each one wanted his piece of the action. I said that I was a cotton broker and didn't care who won the fight, so long as the citizens received good care. We looked at peoples' qualifications and placed them according to need rather than academic degree. Then we set up a single system for record keeping and case reporting. Nobody had any monopoly.

"If I had been a professional person, somebody would have had me fired, but there were four of us businessmen and three bankers on the board. We figured out what was needed for the community, which was cooperation. Now most of the professionals like it that way too."

The work of this citizen went beyond meeting with professionals. He had to persuade some women that their favorite charity was being supported rather than destroyed. Local property owners had to be reassured that "satellite" mental health centers in all neighborhoods would stabilize a community. Some angry blacks had to see the specific plans and budgets for programs in the ghetto and compare them with other parts of town.

The establishment of satellite centers is part of a third responsibility that we accept as citizens. This is the duty to keep the doors open for troubled people. It is so easy to appropriate the money for one clinic in a hospital and then assume that we have reached out to help all the unfortunates.

This was the assumption of planners for one clinic in a downtown hospital. But when a management consultant evaluated the relationship of the institution to the community, he found that only one person in a thousand had any contact with the hospital program in mental health; yet there were thousands of transients coming into the area around the hospital each year, and ethnic groups were continually complaining that no one met their needs.

The hospital then cooperated with a community action committee to establish storefront centers for mental health in a dozen parts of the hospital's patient catchment area. The workers in these centers were recruited from their own neighborhoods. They spoke the language of the ethnic group that they served. Within a year, records showed that one out of every four persons in the catchment area had some contact with the mental health program. When citizens extended the clinic beyond the hospital, they increased its ministry one-hundred fold.

But the very expansion of services can create problems. Who will pay for all this extra help? Federal funds are generous in the beginning, but they decrease every year. Citizens must persuade their city or county to appropriate necessary funds to match and then take over the budgets for mental health. This is a fourth area of responsibility, which calls for some difficult decisions. There may be fifty to one hundred agencies on the tax rolls that request assistance. Why should mental health have priority?

The survival of the center programs will depend on the

lives they have touched. One physician told of the experience in his county when federal funds declined. The county was poor and could only make up half of the amount necessary to pay the salaries of five workers in a mental health center. One landowner, whose grandson had "blossomed" in a progressive mental retardation program, contributed the necessary funds for salaries during that year. Other persons, who had seen new happiness in their own families, began to speak for an upward evaluation of property taxes to insure county funds for salaries in the next fiscal year. One man said to a tax commissioner: "I know it will cost me money, and it will be the same for you. But if you could see the change in the life of my father, who was becoming an alcoholic, you would know that the clinic is worth all that we put into it."

As a Volunteer

People put money where their lives are. Some people can support a program through tax dollars, others make voluntary contributions of money or time. For most centers, the contribution of time is most appreciated. The hours that a person contributes to some community agency is the best way that we show a staff that their work is appreciated.

One county seat town did not have the necessary tax base to support a large mental health center, but they could afford a social worker, a part-time psychologist from a neighboring college, two nurses and several mental health aides.

The social worker told church and civic clubs that the clinic staff was happy to be recognized with new publicity, but could not handle all of the calls that came in because they were becoming known. The most difficult problem was the increase in calls for help from people who thought of suicide. Several church and civic leaders organized a twenty-four hour telephone service for suicide prevention under the guidance of the center staff. A prominent social leader made this her project for the year. Forty persons received training as crisis counselors and manned the service without professional assistance. At the end of two years, the group had brought hope and help to many persons by phone. They had also come into contact with a far wider range of human problems than any of them would have met in their daily work. They were a wiser and more sympathetic group of helpers.

Most of the volunteers in suicide prevention were mature persons. Some of them were retired. Others were housewives. What kind of service is available for the youth? One answer was found in a summer camping program for disturbed children. The students of one college provided most of the staff for a series of outings during the summer. The children were delighted, and the students were amazed by what they learned. One said: "I thought that every kid would run down to the water and jump in. I had been trained in water safety and knew how to arrange games for children, but we spent all day getting some of those boys and girls into the water. It was a major celebration when one got his head wet. It takes lots of patience, but I am learning."

Camping and swimming are examples of the wide range of recreation and occupational skills that can be provided by volunteers. A retired gardener brought greenery into every corner of a hospital with his hours of free time in an institution's greenhouse. Patients loved to learn from him to grow flowers. They triumphantly took their seedlings back to the wards for display. Many of these patients remarked that they had never grown anything before in their lives.

The women of several church groups organized homemaking classes for women who were returning to their city from a state mental hospital. Soon they found that the classes were also needed for the women who were outpatients at a neighboring mental health center. In recruiting for the project, a woman told her friend: "You can't imagine what it's like to have no instruction in cooking. But I meet women every day who can only do one thing, fry steak. So every Friday, when the husband comes home with his money, they go to the grocery store and buy steak. It is eaten in two days and they live on bread for the rest of the week. They are just amazed to learn that leftovers can go into a casserole."

There are so many of these ordinary skills in life that we take for granted. But many of them have not been shared with the people who come to mental health centers. No one had the time, or took the time to play with them, teach them, enjoy them. These are the little things in life that we can contribute to their renewal.

As a Staff Member

Volunteers are often recruited by friends who are paid workers in a clinic or hospital. When the community trusts the recommendations of staff members, there are more referrals to the center, more volunteers to help and more money for expanded programs.

People always want the "inside story" on public agencies, especially new and untried ones. I have often found during the discussion period of a Sunday School lesson that people want to ask general and specific questions about my work in mental health. I had thought that as the visiting preacher for that day I would be used entirely as a clergyman. But people want information about the way in which professionals help others, and recommendations on how people can help their friends or family members.

In one church a young lady began to answer questions along with me during a Sunday School discussion. When I asked, she told the class that she worked on the children's unit of a nearby state mental hospital. "Oh, I didn't know that you did that kind of work," said several women in the class, and then there was new attention to this member who had been quietly listening to others in the past. For fifteen minutes she lead the discussion on work with the parents of disturbed children. At the close of the hour, people not only expressed gratitude for her instruction, but also said that they now knew what was going on in "those strange new buildings."

A staff member can be an excellent teacher and public relations person for his clinic to the church and community. At the same time, his church membership and basic philosophy of life can make a contribution in the work-a-day affairs of a hospital. I saw this in a social worker who "kept her cool" as a mental health clinic was being expanded. There were many jurisdictional disputes between professional people in private agencies, city and county welfare, local hospitals, and the mental health center. When a supervisor praised her for sitting calmly through an abusive administrative conference, she replied: "Well I guess I'm a tough old bird. These are good people. I see them in my church or know their families. They just get uptight about a new organization with some bright aggressive professionals telling people what to do. But we'll work it out."

This lady says nothing in her professional work that would increase tension between anxious groups. When she wants to say what she really feels about things, she sits down with her Sunday School teacher and his wife, who is a social worker. The three of them can laugh about the human comedy of well-trained people who can be just as anxious as anyone else.

Christian faith is probably of most help to a staff member when confronting the problem of evil. Everyday we see unexplainable tragedies, entrenched selfishness, unnecessary conflict. Faith does not explain physical or moral evil, but it does transcend it. We believe there is something more than meets the eye in this life. There is a God who suffers with us in the tragedies of our times.

Faith not only offers strength to rise above circumstances, it also keeps us from being too surprised and shattered by evil close at hand. A staff is often shaken by the suicide of a director, the divorce of a devoted doctor, the growing jealousy and defensiveness of an experienced unit leader toward some new consultant or staff member.

These are the expected reactions of fallible men. Christianity teaches tolerance for human weakness. "All have sinned and come short of the glory of God."

Unfortunately, the faith that should make us wise and serene in the presence of human failure, may be twisted into Pharisaical shock and condemnation. This is the legalism that we have examined in earlier chapters. It is the poorest possible preparation for work with people under stress.

The better way of faith is forgiveness. We recognize that people are limited in their patience, acceptance of competitors, and ability to give and give and give to distressed people all day long. The biblical command is to bear one another's burdens. This fulfils the law of Christ.

As a Church Member

Organizations as well as individuals must "bear one another's burdens." Clinics need churches to help them care for people, to plan creative services, to support needed programs with political and professional groups. Neither organization can carry the burden of troubled people alone.

In a Texas city, this cooperation began when women of the church began a study of home missions. A recommendation of the program was to visit child care institutions in all parts of the county. On the tour, women saw the noisy confusion of clinics in the ghetto. Mexican mothers came with several preschool children and babies to wait for a physical examination. When the mother was seen by herself, or with one of the children, the rest roamed throughout the building.

The church women took as their project an organization of babysitting for the clinic. In addition to the time that they scheduled, they donated toys, furniture, and their husband's time to paint several rooms in a neighboring building to the clinic.

The women soon found more use for their talents than play with small children. The Mexican and black mothers would sit with the white women as they watched the children and waited for appointments. Soon there were questions: "Where would I go to look for a job?" "How can my son and daughter find a decent job and still go to school?" "Who do I see about the garbage pile in the lot next door?" "Where can I buy clothes that wear well?"

More intimate questions followed as the women met from week to week: "How do I tell my husband that we should not have more babies?" "Do you think that my son could work in a nicer part of town if he graduates from high school?" "Where can I get help for my oldest daughter who is pregnant?"

When the churchwomen asked a doctor and nurse

about these questions, they were assured that this was some of the best help they could offer. People in the ghetto needed help with everyday problems. If someone from the outside treated them with respect and gave them some hope, they might find the strength to get up cheerfully in the morning.

After several months of regular visitation, the wives began to have some questions themselves. These were directed to their husbands and church leaders: "Why doesn't the county buy more space and fix up that clinic?" "When is a social worker going to be added to their staff?" "Who is responsible for garbage collection in that part of town?" "How do we get our streets paved so well and leave holes in the road down by the clinic?" "Why should we spend thousands of dollars to redecorate and furnish our adult Sunday School building when the clinic doesn't even have air conditioning?"

The church began to divert funds from its own physical comfort to the needs of a neglected community. More people gave time as well as money. Two physicians donated one evening a week from their private practice to see working mothers in the clinic. Several retired men began to act as chauffers for mothers and children who were beyond the reach of transportation.

These were direct services to people in another neighborhood. But at the same time, some indirect services were coming to the church that was concerned. Mothers and fathers developed new understanding of the pressures upon youth as the church cooperated in a recreation center for young drug abusers and a "half-way house" for teen-age runaways. Women who had talked with Mexican mothers about the pregnancy of a daughter were able to speak calmly to close friends who found the same problems in a upper class suburb. Businessmen who had condemned relief programs were now more gentle in discussing the failures of life that might come to anyone.

These changes took place in a few of the church members who were very active in the clinic, but their influence spread through church organizations, social groups, and families. The most notable shift was toward a more relaxed evaluation of success. Fathers began to wonder if they should work quite so hard or push their children so straight toward prominent colleges. Mothers saw that some women are happy with their children, whether they comb their hair every hour or walk gracefully. Some of the simple and basic pleasures of living begin to be more important.

When these attitudes are displayed, we have come to a primary answer of the question: What Can I Do About Mental Health as a Christian? We have become in our own being a resource for faith, hope and love. We who have received grace from God can become examples of graciousness.

CHAPTER IX
CAN I HEAL MYSELF?

God's treasure is in earthen vessels. (See 2 Cor. 4:7.) The life of Jesus is manifest in *our* lives. Our personality is the mirror of his grace among men.

What kind of mirror are we? The first chapter of James's epistle contains a warning about people who look at themselves—as in a mirror—and straightway forget what they have seen. These are the double-minded people, unstable in all their ways, who are of no help as a Christian witness.

The Christian witness must know himself. But how is this to be accomplished? One part of the answer is prayer and introspection. A person looks into himself to discover what manner of man he is. He searches the Scriptures and waits for God's guidance in meditation. This is the solitary way toward self-awareness.

The lonely way is not enough. Self-deception rises up to blur our awareness of God's mission for our lives. We select those passages of the Bible that seem convenient and do not even recognize ourselves in other verses.

If you're going to help anyone else toward mental health, start with some attention to your own problems. Almost any believer in the Sermon on the Mount would acknowledge the truth of this warning, but there is wide disagreement on the *way* by which we arrive at self-understanding.

Should I Share?

Some Christians believe that healing is only *within.* They try to be their own mirror. "Isn't it enough for me to talk over my problems with God?" they say. "What place would any other man have in my guidance from the Lord?"

In his most mature writing, Paul describes the Christian experience as the breaking of two barriers: the one between God and man, and the one between man and man. In reconciliation we become adopted sons of God and members of the household of saints. We share with one another in the same family under one Father (Eph. 2:11-21). Who then can say from the Scriptures that he should talk over his faith and his frailty with God *alone?*

Where will we find those people who show us what manner of man we are? Some individuals have learned about themselves through their family life. Parents, aunts and uncles, brothers and sisters pointed out strong and weak places in the self. This is an invaluable source of self-understanding.

But family comments are biased. Even the best of families may not perceive our mission in life. They interpret us in the light of their preconceptions.

We need to go beyond the family for insight. And, if our family provides no self-reflection, we surely need a person or a group who will tell us how we appear to others. With the help of some independent people, we should be able to measure our similarities and differences with others, our strengths and weaknesses, the way we see ourselves, and the way others see us.

Countering the Culture Game

Our secular society increases the need for some group with whom we can be honest. Today's world promotes phony fronts. In the middle class "culture game" of America, men and women strive for the appearance of "normality." We want to be appropriate, to meet all the demands made upon us by families, friends, jobs. We are directed by the desires and standards of others. "They" demand that we be adequate, relaxed, self-assured, happy. Mistakes must be glossed over and doubts concealed.

Where does a person go when he is wearied by reverses in life or doubtful about his abilities? Can he go home? Thousands of miles may separate him from parents, brothers, uncles, lifelong friends. The children may be married and in another city. The wife may be competing with husband as a part of the new liberation.

The great desires of the isolated and successful couple is for some group where they can be themselves without being attacked. They know they are not perfect. Where can they share doubts and fears?

Encounter Groups

Encounter and other human potential groups are being recommended to churches, executive groups, school systems. How can we evaluate the need for such a program, examine the credentials of those who lead, and control the results?

First, do you really want a training session or encounter group? If you know that a changing neighborhood demands better understanding on the part of all people, then a confrontation group may be very helpful. Or if a group of young people in the church are looking for a retreat in which the meaning of faith will come more alive, they may benefit from religiously oriented sensitivity training. If there has just been a change in the chief executives of a denomination, several of these may go with other leaders to a workshop on human relations.

But the problems of your church or organization may not be met by a group of people talking for a weekend. As a school trustee, you may find that morale is low because decision-making is handled in an authoritarian fashion. This is the impediment to communication. People are scared to tell the superintendent what they know is going on. He always takes criticism personally. If you brought principals and superintendent into an encounter group, there would certainly be some feelings expressed! But would the results justify the explosion and resentment? Should poor management be handled by a group of subordinates or by the school board?

A training laboratory at the wrong time or with a vulnerable participant will do more harm than good. In one mental health center, the director asked for staff development workshops, but attended infrequently. Staff members voiced their dissatisfaction with his leadership. He was a good therapist but a poor administrator. The director was unsure of his position anyway. He had hoped that the workshop would make people more sympathetic, easier to work with. Instead, he had to face open opposition that was zeroed in on his most conspicuous weakness—which he would not change.

In contrast, the staff of a large downtown church invited a trainer to lead them in a weekend retreat after the trainer had been with various groups in the church during the week. The trainer summarized for the staff his findings from the week. Some of his remarks caused the pastor to ask if he had shown enough public confidence in one of the assistant pastors. The assistant pastor did not think so. The two men clarified their own feelings about each other, and other staff members fedback their impressions of the relationship of these men to each other, and to the rest of the staff. "Well," said the pastor, "I guess that we would never have cleared this up without some specific focus—and leisure—for this discussion. Thanks."

A second consideration is the *type* of workshop you

CAN I HEAL MYSELF? 123

desire. The church staff wanted an educational experience. They were not in need of therapy. Similarly, many church or couples groups want an enriching and growing group. Suggestions for better relationships are welcomed. They are healthy people with resources to use intelligently and accurately. They readily pick up ideas from each other and use them responsibly.

But if many of the participants are chronically neurotic, the purpose will need to be more therapeutic. Their patterns of living must be untangled and new resources added to their living before they can be restored to health. More time, stricter controls, and specialized leadership will be necessary.

Any of the following groups are helpful *if* you plan ahead and announce the aims for which each is designed:

Enrichment: a series of seminars, or a weekend for healthy people who concentrate on a specific subject, such as family interaction, morals and marriage, teen-agers and parents, faith and doubt, drugs and dependency, or loneliness and companionship. The meeting may be open to any person in your church or organization who seems to have an appropriate interest in the subject, and it may be led by persons with a variety of background and training.

Encounter: sessions in which people from varying social or ethnic groups openly state their prejudices about each other and learn how it feels to walk in another's shoes. Participants should be chosen for their representative function or leadership for potential reconciliation.

Establishment: managerial or professional persons meet

for growth of interpersonal skills which will aid their competence in work. If the people are going to be in the same plant or hospital for the next ten years, they must focus more upon common problems in the job and less upon self-revelations of past history and present prejudices. If they will be scattered after the meeting, the admission of gut-reactions may be more frequent, but there will have to be some covenant about sharing secrets. The leader for these groups is often a person from the profession or business who has had specialized training in leadership development.

Examination: therapy for disturbed people, preceded by psychological consultation and led by a psychiatrist, clinical psychologist, or social worker nurse, or chaplain with graduate training in psychotherapy. The purpose is to examine under skilled leadership the complexities of sick thinking and distorted relationships in a fellowship of concerned people.

After a decision on the type of group you will sponsor, turn to a third issue, the qualifications of persons who will lead the workshop. Look for help from the National Training Laboratories, the American Group Psychotherapy Association, the adult education section of the National Education Association. Any of these organizations may be contacted through your county or state community mental health center, school superintendent, community college, or state university. Several Protestant denominations maintain a staff that recommends personnel or conducts such seminars.

A fourth question is personal, what will *you* gain from sponsoring or attending these sessions? If you wish to know yourself better, to gain more understanding of those with whom you will work, then the first three types of seminar will be appropriate. If, on the other hand, you are really worried about yourself, seek some professional guidance on the type of group which you should enter. Psychotherapy may be recommended, either individually or in a group. Or, you may find that your fears are unfounded. You're not sick, just lonely and confused. The shocks of life are showing, and you need some reassessment through a caring fellowship organized for renewal. It is this type of enrichment, the renewal group, that has become very popular in churches.

What's in a Group?

When you enter some form of group workshop, you may wonder what is expected. What is a "group" experience, anyway?

Any group will begin with a focus on interaction. There will be some deliberate concentration on the way we talk, our tone of voice, the person or persons to whom we address ourselves, the way in which we sit, the place where we sit, the movements we make, the expressions that show on our face.

A second characteristic of a group is a sense of direction. People will soon discuss the reasons for their assembly. Usually the purpose is to relate with more accuracy and sympathy.

If it is a therapy group, the object will be more intimate. In psychotherapy, patients have two paramount problems for which help is sought: (1) difficulty in establishing and maintaining friendship, marriage, or any warm relationship, and (2) difficulty in developing and maintaining a sense of self-esteem. The group experience usually offers such people a sense of acceptance despite failings, an opportunity to talk freely and honestly, a chance to show interest and understanding of others, and support from others during trying times and conspicuous blunders.

A group is also defined by the boundaries and limitations that are agreed on in early sessions. If the group is theme-centered, you will agree to begin with one topic and to discuss it only in relation to your feelings and those of others in this circle. If the purpose is therapeutic, there are questions of confidence to be settled.

A fourth characteristic of group experience is the emergence of dominant, dependent, helpful, withdrawn, humorous, and antagonistic characteristics. These are roles that become visible as the group develops. As you observe one of these traits in the person beside you, or when others see it in you, you can better evaluate your role back home as parent, child, spouse, student, or worker.

A final mark of group development is mutual attraction. The people really care for each other. If someone is absent, others ask why. If a member is hurting, his fellows want to know what has happened and how they may help. When one person shares a success in personal development, others rejoice with him.

This ability to bear one another's burdens is built upon self-knowledge and sacrifice. The sacrifice is of pride and conceit. We can help others when we are willing to say that we need help also. Then we can see the problem *with* a person, instead of looking down on him or offering some inappropriate advice or hasty action. This is the principle that has made Alcoholics Anonymous successful and has recently been applied in Synanon and related problems for drug addicts. It can be generally extended to all types of sharing groups. Young people are less compulsive in their attempts to help others when they have first found acceptance for their own strivings toward competence. Older persons can comfort one another with understanding and love after they are first free from the burden of guilt for their own failings in the past. When we are free, we can allow freedom to others when we offer assistance.

What are the rewards of sharing in a responsible fellowship? We are offered acceptance and approval for our moves toward stronger affirmation of healthy tendencies in ourselves. Because of the values we find in ourselves, we can suppress some of the undesirable qualities of personality that have hampered us in the past. The rewards of openness, trust, and warmth are greater than the lures of secrecy, distrust, and deviousness. We also receive specific understanding of our ways of thinking and the steps by which people go through the solution of problems. With this understanding we can approach our own difficulties with new confidence and provide wise counsel to those who lean upon us.